Romano Guardini

THE FOCUS OF FREEDOM

translated by Gregory Roettger, O.S.B.

HELICON
Baltimore—Dublin

Helicon Press, Inc.
1120 N. Calvert Street, Baltimore, Md. 21202

Helicon Limited
20 Upr. Fitzwilliam Street, Dublin 2, Ireland

Library of Congress Catalog Card Number 65-15038

Originally published in German by Verlag der Arche, Zurich, Switzerland, under the titles *Der Heilige Franziskus* (1951), *Vom Sinn der Gemeinschaft* (1950), *Vom Sinn der Schwermut* (1949), and *Lebendiger Geist* (1950).

PRINTED IN THE REPUBLIC OF IRELAND

CONTENTS

3

C. 1

ST. FRANCIS AND SELF-ACHIEVEMENT

Every truly perceptive person recognizes in his life one process that is full of wonder. That process brings to his attention in a special manner the thought of providence. We may think of providence in terms of particular events; but these are supplementary, exterior. In a far more exalted sense, providence finds expression in the entire course of a man's personal growth. A man matures according to his own nature and, by being himself, becomes a guide and a liberator of others. By developing his own innermost being, he articulates the deepest sentiments of others. He becomes a word for those who are united with him in some special community of existence or mode of life. Providence, understood in this sense, is deeply rooted in man's being; complete autonomy and a most profound sense of destiny achieve an inexpressible union.

St. Francis was such a man. In him, this union was achieved. In him, the purity of free personal growth became the liberating word and directive form for many.

I have followed St. Francis in the land where he lived and in the traditions that have been handed down about him. I have striven for impartiality; as I have seen his figure, I shall present it. This will not be a disquisition on "St. Francis and Our Times." I shall deal solely with him, and—in the only way consonant with the mystery that he is—without any distinct purpose in mind. If, however, he does find a place in our age, if that *communio* to which we referred unites him with us, then we ought to turn to him in great simplicity and apply to ourselves the word in him that is addressed to us.

II

A traveller goes south from Padua by way of Ferrara and

Bologna, and ascends the Apennines to the height of the passes, to that unforgettable spot where, in a flood of light, the Tuscan plains open before him. He then descends to Pistoia and Florence. By-passing Arezzo, he skirts the heights of Cortona and by way of the shore of Lake Trasimene arrives at Perugia. On this journey, despite the plethora of beauty and of history that colors the entire region, he will be struck by one thing in particular : beginning with Bologna, the form of the structures changes. Houses, farm buildings, cities become different. Baroque flourishes in Venezia. There is a pleasing softness in the manner in which the flat surfaces are bordered, one against another, or the mass of one house against that of another. Everything is artistic, and despite the clarity of the disposition, a subtle indeterminateness hovers over the forms, allowing room for the delicate play of things not yet become set, of things still in movement and flow. Suddenly a profound change occurs in the style of construction, in the manner of conception and execution. The style assumes a plastic character. The corners become sharper, the masses more definitely defined. On the slopes of the Apennines toward Tuscany the houses lie four-square, cast about like cubical dice. And when at last the traveller stands on the heights opposite Perugia, it seems as if on the other side crystal rises above crystal.

True, architecture first strikes the eye of the beholder ; but that is merely the means of ingress. Actually, it is perceived with the body, with the curve of the forehead, with the expansiveness of the breast, with the whole vital being of the one who walks through the built-up spaces. Suddenly the viewer is struck by something very elementary ; here all hardness is formed and stratified. Wood, plaster, and ornamentation disappear. Only stone remains. Here is a triumph of stone, of the hard, calcareous stone of those hills with its sharp profiles and deep luminosity. He is struck, too, by the manner of building, by the complete absence of affectation, of decoration, of *chiaroscuro*. Everywhere he looks, there are only exact surfaces, transparent masses, clear relationships. Everything is plastic, cubical. The majesty of stone reigns in unrivalled triumph. One sees it when passing along the *Maestà delle Volte*. Imagine a street being called "The Majesty of the Arches." And truly there is majesty in the way the arches swing from house to house. When one enters the houses on the site of the old castle, or goes into the courts and gazes at the gigantic prisms rising upward; when one climbs the street and senses the hewn stonework surrounding him, and then becomes aware of the breadth and height of the space rising above the disciplined masses—then there is an urge to shout at such bold declaration of strength.

Assisi is smaller, friendlier, almost childlike one might say, in comparison to the dark power of the ancient Etruscan city. Still, it all grew out of the same blood. Its smallness covers a hidden greatness. Here, too, one sees the hewn hardness of stone, row on row ; here, too, the simple cubical masses ; here, too, the marvellous wedding of form with the expansiveness of space. The city is built on the slope of the hill ; almost all the streets ascend. The plan has a peculiar openness about it. When I compare it with the hill cities of Venezia, it seems to me that Assisi has no dark corners, no secrecy, that every form stands forth freely in the light and the pure air. Again and again the streets emerge into small squares, and the wide view of the Umbrian plain meets the eye. Everywhere the cool air moves and washes every form with purity. And when the sun stands over the city and the air shimmers and the stone glistens, suffused with light, when this entire picture of hewn corners and masonry masses stands in the soughing purity of wind and brilliant sun-light—then the soul is touched by the mystery of great depth, depth which consists not of chaos but of clarity. It is so simple that words fail to describe it, yet so impenetrable that it cannot be grasped.

But if a man looks afield, a marvellous panorama beckons him. The Umbrian plain extends from Perugia to Spoleto ; the hills rise in a soft light. It is impossible to describe how the power of the form of nearby things, felt in all the fibers of one's being, suddenly stretches out into a great distance of yearning and infinity—without losing itself, without the slightest obscuring of its clarity of outline.

III

Francis grew up in this vital tension which continually renews itself, never disappearing but always overcome by a special attitude of the entire man. A reflection of this tension in the land, composed of human powers, surrounded him and dwelt in his own blood. Bernardone, his father, was a merchant of Assisi. He was securely rooted in the commune, in possessions, and in the law ; a sharp calculator with a hard hand who, when his vital nerve—ambition and wealth—was touched, became a man of ferocious energy. Yet he also took the long view. His affairs often took him far afield. He made many journeys to foreign lands, particularly to the south of France where the most important marts between southern and northern Europe lay. There was something about him that, going beyond figures and wealth, yearned for splendor, for an exalted form of life.

His wife, Pica, a delicate, gentle being, he had brought from Provence. In the year 1182, while he was absent on one of his customary trips, she bore him a son and had him baptized in San Rufino with the name of John. But Bernardone decided to call the boy Francis, summing up, as it were, all his ambitions in his son's name.

St. Francis has been called a romantic. Did not his

father, by giving him the name that refers to the land of
the troubadours, impress this seal upon him for all his life ?

The name was clearly an omen. Francis became a man
in whose soul echoed the call of far places. While living in
the circumscribed present, he always felt the beckoning of
the infinite. His life was a perpetual migration. This might
seem reason enough to number him among the romantics,
among the chronically unstable, the "tramps," the unrealistic, the degenerate. But that is not so ; for Francis belonged
to the sharp corners and the masonry blocks of the Umbrian
houses. He stood in the brilliant light of the Assisi sun.
About him there was nothing vague, nothing complicated or
secretive, nothing muddled. True, for a long time he did not
know what he wanted. The reason, however, was not an
unclear mind or unclear vision, but the fact that he based
his thinking and acting on his maturing life itself. He
limited his knowledge to the degree of his progress. His
grasp of things increased with the process of his growth. As
soon as something revealed itself to him, he possessed it with
perfect clarity. What he received into his soul came forth
from him new and freshly minted. And still his life stretched
into the distance. Still the infinite, existing elsewhere,
vibrated in his lucid present. Still his life was a journey into
the unknown. But his desires did not obfuscate the lucidity
of his view, just as the distinctness of the situation at hand
could never dampen his ardor for flights into the infinite.

So he grew up, like the other children of the city, happy,
vibrant, attractive. No doubt he was soon the leader of the
small group in his quarter of Assisi. He learned what was
taught at the time, reading and writing. Throughout his
life he did not like to write, but preferred to have others
act as his secretaries and then set below his T, the Latin
cross, by way of signature. He was conversant with Latin,

the language of Europe used especially in learned and official circles.

His father was a merchant, and enjoyed a respectable status. He dealt not only in trade goods, but also in things pertaining to the intellectual life. Through him news, new ideas, new impulses filtered through the world. Noblemen did not regard him quite as an equal, but, nevertheless, as a man not far down the social ladder. In Provence, for example, he enjoyed a seminoble status. Bernardone was wealthy, and Francis loved everything that was gay and sparkled with life. He grew out of his children's shoes, but he always remained a center of interest. He was hospitable and generous to a fault, from the fullness of an overflowing heart. As a result the youth of the city, and particularly the aristocratic youth, gathered about him.

And yet he was uncomely in appearance, small, in fact and, according to the legend, ugly. We recall the passage from the *Fioretti*, where Fra Masseo, beautiful and well-proportioned, cries out, "Why you? Why you? . . . Why do they all run after you? You are neither beautiful nor attractive."

Some see him as merely an unpretentiously joyous man, but this is one of those half-truths by which pious and not-so-pious literature has robbed this truly eminent figure of his greatness. He is regarded as a primitive Brother Jocund, simple as the birds in the trees. But that he certainly was not! True, he prized simplicity very highly, but that does not mean he was a simpleton. He set a distant goal for himself. No creative person is simple, for he is torn between what is and what is to be. Unborn things crowded in on the soul of St. Francis, and he had to pay for them with all those deep sufferings that are the price of producing new life. He was faced with that question of the value of the creative man who is more than he really is, greater than himself and smaller. It is a question of value which consists in this : he who is simply a man, possessed of dignity and his own life, in a very singular way becomes an instrument, a channel, for something else, for the thing to be created. On this point much could still be said.

He was most understanding, and understanding means sympathy, "suffering with" others. From him comes the saying that a man knows only as much as he has suffered. Francis was endowed with an extremely fine sensibility. Many contrasts existed in him, and the important point is that he lived each of them entirely, that he did not try to efface any one of them. He acted on them all. This is a great task. He must have possessed an invincible strength to conquer this situation and to give his life that lucidity which marks all his words and his works.

Thus Francis matured.

In his soul burned an unquenchable desire for great things. He drew his chivalrous ideas of honor, of service to beauty and renown from the tales of his father, from the songs and stories of the troubadours. The ultimate, which for him was poverty, he was to express later by saying that he had espoused Lady Poverty, the most beauteous of all.

He knew that great things were in the offing. At Ponte San Giovanni, he was captured as a twenty-year-old by the Perugians. When the prisoners had languished in captivity for a year and all had lost courage, Francis experienced the triumph of a coming glory. Again and again he closed his narratives with unshakeable faith: "You will see, one day the whole earth will honor me ! " Later, as an escape from great anxiety of heart he attached himself to the suite of a knight of Assisi who planned to join Walter of Brienne in southern Italy to fight for the Guelph cause, and Francis imagined himself in a palace full of arms and splendor.

He was chivalrous—*cortese*. This word cannot be translated, because "courteous" has another meaning now. In its original sense, the word bespeaks a form of life, that of noble behavior. With Francis this noble behavior assumed a deep, inner sweetness, giving it a bell-like character of clarity and beauty.

But accompanying this there was something more. This thoroughly chivalrous man never wished to be a lord. While he belonged to the nobility, he leaned always toward the common folk, fought for their liberty and their rights. He lived at a time when the Guelph movement, the struggle of the citizenry for freedom and power, had gained the upper hand in Italy. At Legnano this young power had conquered the empire. Then came the counterattack under Henry VI. The Ghibellines gained strength, and Conrad, duke of Spoleto, ruled over Assisi as a tyrant from the castle whose ruins even today are impressive. When Innocent III ascended the throne in 1198, Conrad considered his position untenable and submitted to the suzerainty of the Pope. Profiting by his absence, the citizens of Assisi stormed the castle—it is difficult to conceive how they could reduce it to ruins so rapidly—and with incredible speed surrounded the city with mighty walls. Francis was seventeen at the time, and no doubt he savored the passion for liberty to the depths of his being.

The citizenry became conscious of their power. They rose against the nobility, demanded freedom from socage and partition of the estates. The nobility sought aid from their ancient enemy, Perugia, which declared war on Assisi. Francis remained faithful to the citizenry and fought with them as one of the *popolani,* the common folk, as one of the *minori,* the small people. We may see an omen of his future mission in the fact that he reckoned himself among them. After a year peace was concluded. A treaty followed. The rights of the property owners and nobles were re-established;

socage was again imposed on the people. Ten more years passed in this fashion, when Francis stood up anew for the citizenry and helped to bring about a liberating agreement.

Something far deeper than the desire for liberty and social justice drove him to join the oppressed and suffering *minori*. This tendency revealed itself most clearly in his meetings with paupers. Even during the years when he gave his senses full rein and his life was one continuous, brilliant feast, if he happened to come upon a pauper, he was overwhelmed. It was not merely the sight of indigence, but something far more profound that called to him from the poor man.

One day Francis was in his father's emporium. He knew how to sell, tradition assures us ; he had a sense for merchandise and price, a sharp eye and a hand ready to grasp a profit. That is an art, but in Francis it existed side by side with something else. In a moment he could turn about and spend the entire profit on a beautiful cloak or give it to a friend. On this particular day he was standing there, bargaining with a customer, when a poor man entered and began to beg. Francis became impatient and showed him the door. But then commiseration entered his heart. "What if that man had been sent by a duke or a baron to make a request of me. . .?" On the spur of the moment he deserted merchandise and customer to run after the pauper. This showed more than a social sense and a readiness to help. Here we perceive something of the man's nature.

IV

He returned from Perugia and threw himself anew into a tumultuous life, enjoying himself immensely. And those symposia of youth, in which everything was governed by

Francis' *cortesia,* must have sparkled with beauty. Walking the streets of Assisi one evening, I imagined I heard the tumult of youthful spirits, as singing and laughing they set the quiet night ringing. But Francis became so immersed in this life that he fell sick, and for a time he lay at death's door.

This experience affected him deeply. The old, carefree self-assurance left him. Gradually he convalesced, but the disquiet remained. One day—it was spring—he rose and went out through the gate to commune with nature, hoping in this way to find himself again. He followed a secret oscillation that determined his entire life ; one pole lay in the city, the other in nature. He sought the life-giving powers of the earth to renew his strength. He sought them now, but there was no response. The void that had opened in him remained ; in fact, it grew deeper. He did not understand himself any longer. Neither did his parents or his friends understand him. Francis took the only step left to him. Again he threw himself into his former life.

Soon a new plan engaged his attention, the journey to Walter of Brienne in Apulia. Expectation and impatience tormented him. He garbed himself so splendidly that the whole city spoke of it—only to give everything to a poor knight shortly before the departure date. Again and again he repeated, "I know that one day I will be a great prince." He set out, but on the way, at Spoleto, a fever prostrated him. And then a dream shattered the attraction of worldly knighthood.

"Where are you going?" a voice asked.

"To Apulia, to become a knight."

"Now tell me, Francis, which of the two would be of greater advantage to you, the master or the servant?"

"The master!"

"Why then do you leave the master for the sake of the servant, the prince for the vassal?"

Francis turned back. The entire city mocked him. His father grew furious at being thus compromised. And again Francis immersed himself in the old life.

But the void in his soul deepened. A time of painful searching began. He found a sympathetic friend. Some conjecture that it was the later Elias of Cortona, the man who, in opposition to Francis and with the cooperation of Cardinal Hugolin, gave a moderate tendency to the Order. If it was he, then this meeting was a symbol of tragic proportions.

Francis carried his misery out into nature, by lonely paths into a cave near Assisi. He wanted to know what he should do, what was expected of him, what moved and urged him on so mysteriously.

One day he invited his friends to dinner. They made him king of the feast. At the end of the meal the group stormed through the night, their song and tumult echoing in the streets. The year was 1205; he had attained his twenty-third year. The *Legenda Trium Sociorum* says that he walked in the midst of his companions, carrying the sceptre of his joyous kingship in his hand. Yet he moved more slowly, lagged behind them, became pensive. Then suddenly it happened. God touched his heart: "Behold, on the instant the Lord visited him, and such great sweetness filled his heart that he could neither move nor speak, and could feel or perceive nothing but that sweetness."

The companions noticed that he was no longer with them; they returned "and saw with amazement how he had changed into a completely different person." They asked, "What were you thinking of ? . . . Are you perhaps intending to get married?" But he replied, most likely in a tone they had never heard before, "You have spoken correctly. I was

2

thinking of taking as my bride the noblest, the most beauteous, and the richest lady you have ever seen."

Here we see the first breakthrough of that spiritual rebirth in God as a result of which his soul, dedicated to pain and blessedness, was to open its doors for good. True, he would remain subject to all human weaknesses; and yet, in accord with the words of Isaiah, he will be like an iron wall against everything that threatens his vocation.

The event caused a rift between Francis and his friends. They drew back, and he no longer sought their company. He felt that he must divest himself of everything. He sought solitude, so that what had begun on that memorable evening might become clear to him. Francis never lived by principle, never set up a theory regarding his life. He simply went ahead, experienced, acted. As a result of what had been manifested to him, he now took the first step. Once he had taken it the second followed, and so it went on. And always he impressed a definite character on all he did. Everything became vital, distinct, sharply defined.

It must indeed have been a wonderful time when he wandered through the solitude of the Umbrian countryside, listening for what was to come, sorrowing for everything that had gone before, but still facing the future with expectation and confidence.

The bond between him and the poor drew tighter. They came always closer to him. He felt community with them; he thought of himself as united to them in a mysterious way.

One day as he rode forth, a leper was standing by the roadside and called to him. These unfortunates had always inspired him with horror. With simultaneous sympathy and terror his heart had revolted against the dreadfulness of their fate. So it happened also on this occasion, and he turned his horse away. Suddenly he realized what he had done, wheeled his horse about, sprang from the saddle, gave the leper all the money he had with him, and kissed his hand.

Here we see a new breakthrough—not into social action, not into the realm of active compassion, but into the mystery of suffering. Into the mystery that reveals itself in pain seen in relation to the cross. The pain against which the heart rebels, while at the same time recognizing it as the ultimate verity.

All that happened tended to further estrange his friends. They no longer took him seriously, feeling possibly that here was a seriousness of which they wanted no part. His father, too, turned away from him. He had patiently borne and financed the escapades of bygone years since they catered to his pride. But that his son should now shun everything, that he should tramp the fields and hide out in caves like a man losing his mind—this he could not bear. A great loneliness surrounded Francis.

But his interior life continued to grow stronger.

Near Assisi lay a small, half-ruined chapel, sacred to the memory of St. Damian. An old crucifix hung on one of its walls. Francis casually entered the place while on one of his solitary rambles. With all his heart he prayed that God might enlighten him; his entire inner being was ready. He looked at the face of the Crucified; it moved and he heard divine words. He understood that Christ accepted his oblation of self, and an unspeakable fervor invaded his soul.

There, in the depths of that encounter with the Crucified, in the act of becoming one with Christ in suffering, the seed of a new existence germinated.

Indeed, he was not the lyrical Brother Jocund, nor was he a pantheist at one with the world. The root of his whole existence lay in the awful and sweet mystery of God's love, whose expression is the cross. This mystery overwhelmed the soul of St. Francis and drew him into itself for good: "From that hour," says the *Legenda,* "his heart was pierced and afire with the memory of the Lord's Passion." All that he was, all that he did, all the results that were achieved because of him, had their origin here.

It again was a symbol of profound meaning (a point to which we shall return later). This hour saw his soul united to Christ by a bond that was never more to be broken. This was the hour when the foundation was laid for that to which he adhered to his dying day, namely, that he had been "taught by God himself." This hour issued in the command: "Francis, do you not see how my house is falling into ruin? Go and repair it." My house, the church! First he took this directive literally, as he did everything that happened to him. He thought it referred to the church of San Damiano which indeed was in a ruinous condition. That was the step he was to take now. But soon he would understand that something far more profound was meant than that little sanctuary, namely, the living Church.

Immediately he threw himself into the task at hand. For the more urgent needs he gave the priest the money he had with him. Then he hurried home, gathered together a number of bolts of cloth, mounted, and rode to Foligno. He sold everything, including the horse, and returned to give the proceeds to the priest. But he, fearing difficulties, rejected the money. Francis threw the useless stuff into a corner. He himself remained at San Damiano. Bernardone was disturbed and sought him everywhere, anger, disappointment, and love contending within his soul. Francis learned of his father's search and, fearing the worst, he hid himself.

But then he felt the dictate of honor. A knight may not flee. And so he went to Assisi. We can imagine his appearance. The intervening period of austerities and interior struggles had doubtlessly taken a terrible toll of this man who was by nature delicate. The people regarded him as demented; they ran together and mocked him. His father heard of it and, beside himself with fury, locked Francis in a dark room. After a few days Bernardone had to depart. At once the mother released her son, who immediately returned to San Damiano. His father sought him there, only to hear Francis declare that he was a servant of Christ and need not accept any further orders from him. At that the father cited him to court. Francis appealed to the spiritual arm and appeared before the bishop's tribunal in the square before the church of Santa Maria Maggiore. The bishop advised him to renounce his inheritance in order to pacify Bernardone. Without a word Francis retired to a room of the episcopal residence. He returned stark naked, lay his clothes at the foot of the judge, and said, "Listen, all of you, and understand it well: hitherto I have called Peter Bernardone my father. But since I am now resolved to serve the Lord, I return to him the money about which he is so overwrought as well as all the clothes that are my inheritance. In the future I will say, 'Our Father, who art in heaven,' and no longer, 'Father Peter Bernardone.' "

The father, in a paroxysm of wrath and grief, snatched up the clothes and money and departed. But the bishop enfolded the trembling Francis in his cloak.

This event defies description. Interior resolution and exterior execution form a unity. Something irrevocable had happened.

Francis went forth out of the city into the springtime air. Unable to contain himself in the face of the overwhelming power of divine life that broke forth in him, he sang. He sang the songs of the troubadours.

This occurrence is immense and illuminating. In its light we understand clearly what had happened in San Damiano: nothing stood between God and Francis any longer. He belonged entirely to God and God entirely to him, and that says all.

Poverty, which from his youth had touched his heart in the person of the poor, became the form of this more intimate relationship, so that henceforth he could truly say, "Our Father, who art in heaven . . ." Poverty is the form of liberty in God. Francis wanted to be completely free, free for God. Nothing between him and God. And poverty became the expression of this relation.

Not that the world had become abhorrent to him. Surely the song of the birds never sounded sweeter to him than when he left the piazza of Santa Maria Maggiore and mounted the slope of Monte Subasio under the budding trees. His poverty was liberty.

This liberty was love. Not primarily the liberty of the intellect, which can deliberate; not primarily the liberty of the will, which attains to freedom by systematic practice; but rather direct love, acting in the power of a heart touched by God.

For that reason we need see nothing negative in all this; everything is "yes." Everything burgeons and glistens and vibrates with life.

Here we have the great act of seeing eye-to-eye with God.

From this eye-to-eye encounter with God springs an attitude of openness to creatures. The heart, now liberated and enlightened, can turn its gaze again to the earth, and the marvel of Franciscan "brother"-hood comes into being. Francis could now say "you" to all things. He looked into their faces, into their hearts: "Brother Sun," 'Brother Fire," "Brother Death" and "Brother Man." No, more correctly, "You, Brother Bernard and Sister Clara." A curious feeling overcomes a man when he stands at Francis' grave and says to himself, "Here rests the heart that experienced such a marvel."

From such a heart comes the word that is understood. It is not learnèd, not pedagogically prudent, not artificially contrived. It is life, pure love of God.

And when that precious element is added, that gift of God which is beauty of soul; when an inner melody pervades everything, so that what the heart experiences again and again bursts forth in song; when a wondrous sweetness fills everything—then it happens that men simply follow him and no longer can loosen their hearts from him.

V

And now we should describe how a new life broke forth from this fiery root. How Francis wandered about; how he sought solitude and then returned to the company of men; how people listened eagerly to his word and therein found the answer to their questioning and seeking. We ought to speak of the gentle fraternal relationship he established between man and man; of his deep, vigorous, holy spirit of liberty formed in accord with God's will; of his nearness to God, and of the vibrant religious power that speaks directly, from the present life. Everywhere, he moved people to action. In his presence all the beneficent powers of generosity, of love, of the creative and transforming might of the heart were aroused. He brought peace to families, to city and to country, which before had been torn with hatred and enmity. The power of this entirely selfless love and the presence of God, the influence of his direct relationship to everything that lives, also embraced nature—the beasts, the birds, the wolf. His way of life and his words enkindled fellowship, and companions flocked to him; they gave away everything and followed him.

We should speak, too, of the ineffable purity and beauty that the name Clare evokes. At the age of eighteen, she came to him, and he, in the sovereignty of his knowledge and his union with God, disregarded all social conventions and received her into the new community. She would turn out to be the most faithful of all. In her his spirit lived on, pure and deep, for many years after his death. Indeed, one might even say that Clare lived the spirit of Francis more purely—or at least more clearly—than it was possible, in the tumult of struggle, for Francis himself to live it. To this very day an unexcelled image of what Francis was like is revealed in the miniscule choir in which Clare and her sisters at San Damiano prayed. That spot, with its miserable benches and seats and shabby lecterns, bespeaks such perfect poverty, and is at the same time so thoroughly human while breathing such a spiritual atmosphere, that the visitor is forced to his knees and to the acknowledgment that he is in the presence of something that ranks among the noblest things on this earth.

Of all this and much else we ought to speak. But one trait of St. Francis, without which his image would be false, still must be mentioned. Hitherto, reference frequently has been made to the strong contrasts that existed side by side in him. Possibly his greatness is revealed best in the fact that he did not try to reconcile these contrasts, but carried out entirely those on one side as well as those on the other. His foundation was so deep, his life so genuine, that the contrarieties, far from remaining merely opposing entities, merged into a living union. For this reason he merits credence. For this reason he is worthy of trust, because he so clearly experienced the powers that everywhere exist side by side and in opposition to one another.

What affected him most powerfully, however, and

filled him with a sense of both grandeur and pain, was the contrast between his interior life and the Church.

Even when he came to write his testament, Francis stressed the point that in all things affecting his mission, "no one taught me what I should do; but he himself, God the All-Highest, revealed to me that I had to live according to the norm of the holy Gospel." But the next sentence continues, "I had this Rule written in few and simple words, and the Pope confirmed it." The preceding sections contain an appreciation of the Church, of the priestly office, and of the Sacrament that is deeply moving in its stark simplicity. Here the two realities—"the two" puts it badly and crudely, but emphasizes what is meant—stand clearly revealed side by side. And it must not be forgotten that we are speaking of his testament, a document written many years after the trying struggle begotten by that contrast. We can trace the tension back to the moment of the event at San Damiano, when he entered that close union with Christ which was later to be perfected on the lonely heights of Verna— unconditional oneness with Christ. The words Christ then addressed to him, which condense the significance of the moment, were as follows: "Do you not see how my house is falling into ruin? Go and repair it!"

We sense the import of this command. This is not a question of the Church as a merely juridical institution enforcing its laws with regard to the individual who could and might live by his own inner freedom and fullness. Here stands the Church, objectively, expressing the universality of everything Christian, independent of the individual. Not only does it stand before the individual; it exists in him. And he, closely united to God, is exhorted to safeguard the seriousness of his spiritual rebirth by his work in the Church.

The germinal and essential form of this relationship now began to evolve.

Francis initiated a new life as a result of his fundamental experience. Everything must be directed toward God; he must be completely free for him. Consequently he had to deprive himself of all possessions—and "possessions" meant to him not only wealth and property, but also learning, worldly prudence, relationships, rights, and privileges. This impulse proved to be of irresistible power. First scattered individuals, then increasing numbers of men and women flocked to him and entered his community. He demanded that they divest themselves of everything, that they rely solely on confidence in God. The manner in which he tried them, the form in which he received them, the entire system by which he governed the brothers and sisters, proceeded from the inspiration of his religious consciousness. Ever greater grew his influence over the people. The *fratres minores* preached everywhere, and their word, pregnant with power and supported by the charismatic atmosphere that surrounded them, made a tremendous impression.

Inevitably, the means of directing these energies became a problem. Francis was convinced that the Gospel and the few directives he had first formulated would suffice. They certainly sufficed for him, a man who lived by the unity of his inner experience. But he forgot to what measure most men are dominated by their environment, the thousand concrete situations of life that would have to be regulated by those general directives, and what power of creative application of the general rules to ever new circumstances he was expecting from so many individuals.

Near Assisi, in the *carceri* on Monte Subasio so beloved by Francis, I saw the stone chamber, narrow as a coffin, in which he was wont to sleep. I also saw the cells—though they really are not cells, but only a few rocks piled up to provide shelter from the most inclement weather or simple excavations in which a man can scarcely stand upright—in which many brothers lived for years on end. I was roused from my reverie by the words of my companion, "Is not something like that below human dignity?" And I understood that the poverty that Francis desired presupposes a charism. Such detachment from everything demands a continually effervescent interior religious life which regards exterior things not only as expendable, but as actually obstructive. But what if this spirit no longer gushes forth? It is too facile a solution to say that this is precisely the tragedy of the religious life and that it must be lived absolutely. For genuine religion, which seeks men's salvation, takes into account not only the absolute, but also the possible. And the "great ones" bear a heavy responsibility, by reason of the precept imposed by Christ in referring to the "little ones, who may not be scandalized." As far as liberty is concerned, where does genuine liberty, really founded on God's will, cease and insubordination, self-deception, and spiritual quixotism begin? Particularly in the case of souls of such ardor and creative imagination as that of St. Francis?

At this point in the history of the Order, the Church took a stand contrary to the personal experience and personal conviction of its founder. Cardinal Hugolini joined forces with Elias of Cortona, to whom Francis had confided guidance of the Order. (Earlier I pointed out the significant coincidence that it seems to have been this Elias who, in the time of the first crisis, sympathetically supported Francis.) They forced upon Francis, despite his strong opposition, the degree of cohesion, order, and accommodation to the sociological structure, of striving after culture, worldly goods, and learning, that appeared to them necessary in order to channel this violent flood, which might just as easily have spread ruin as blessing.

Therefore, this seems to have been the heroic and grand element in Francis: he did not believe that this accommodation of his original design was necessary; he held to the idea of a complete detachment from everything, of a radical and exclusive dependence on God, for the entire Order and for all time; but he heard the command of the Church and he obeyed it. A soldier can still grasp the meaning of that, and perhaps a few others who know what command and obedience signify—that is, the genuine article, not some theoretical proposition. This sort of thing has been largely forgotten. The individual is faced with a reality which receives its validity not from his judgment but from God and bears the seal of Christ's authority: "He who hears you, hears me." As a result, the individual must admit that this reality has been legitimated by God, that it is truly the "Church." Once he has recognized this fact and given his adherence, he need not investigate in particular cases whether its command is correct. As soon as that command has been legitimately promulgated, he is bound. In fact, he cannot always perceive its correctness, for here he is faced with the formal universal reality to which his individual judgment must yield. This calls for obedience in its most difficult and most exalted form: blind obedience. It bears within itself the tension that was expressed once for all and sanctified by the words uttered in Gethsemane, "Father, if it is possible, let this cup pass away from me; yet not as I will, but as thou willest."

By reason of the mystery inherent in God's kingdom, a man's life has two focal points: himself as an individual and the whole, the Church. These cannot be deduced one from the other; both are independent. Both point to an ultimate goal, a single goal. But their paths cannot be plotted. Sometimes they approach one another to the point of almost merging; but it always remains an "almost." The tension persists. Occasionally, however, they diverge very widely, and then it seems as if the individual must collapse under the weight of the strangeness and harshness that threatens him.

Only he who understands this can grasp the true greatness of Francis. Oneness with the Crucified here finds its
extreme consequence. The Lord has said, "Unless the grain
of wheat fall into the ground and die, it remains alone." The
tremendous impulse set in motion by Francis, the living seed
planted by him, was indeed destined to fructify, but he had
to die. Possibly he was fated to retain his original concept
and intention to the end. Possibly he was not granted a
knowledge of the synthesis, so that the seed might be placed
in the ground with undiminished vitality. Then the accommodation would have taken place over his head, accepted
indeed by him in blind obedience, but without his com-
prehending its meaning.

VI

In the upper valley of the Arno lies a mountain called La
Verna. Count Orlando had given it to Francis. It is a solitary
eminence, its slopes covered with fragrant woods full of
singing birds; the summit affords a panoramic view of
Romagna, of the sea, of Umbria and Tuscany. After the
painful struggles of the past years, Francis went there in
1224, two years before his death. Three of the most faithful
of his earliest followers accompanied him—Fra Masseo, Fra
Angelo, and Fra Leone.

At the time Francis was already sick. He knew that he
did not have long to live. He yearned for a period of perfect
solitude and intense prayer. He had his associates construct
for him a hut of branches apart from them, and on the feast
of the Assumption of our Lady, August 15, he entered into
the silence of prayer. Once during the day and once during
the night Brother Leo visited him and brought him bread
and water. The days and the nights passed in a solitude with
God, the profundity and ardor of which the existing narra-

tives give us only a hint. Then came September 14, the feast of the Exaltation of the Cross.

St. Bonaventure described the event that occurred on that day: "When, therefore, by seraphic glow of longing he had been uplifted toward God, and by his sweet compassion had been transformed into the likeness of him who of his exceeding love endured to be crucified . . . , while he was praying on the side of the mountain, he beheld a seraph having six wings, flaming and resplendent, coming down from the heights of heaven . . . There appeared betwixt the wings the figure of a man crucified, having his hands and feet stretched forth in the shape of a cross, and fastened unto a cross . . . As the vision disappeared, it left in his heart a wondrous glow, but on his flesh also it imprinted a no less wondrous likeness of its tokens. For forthwith there began to appear in his hands and feet the marks of the nails, even as he had just beheld them in the figure of the crucified . . . The right side, moreover, was—as if it had been pierced with a lance—seamed with a ruddy scar.

"Francis himself, albeit he strove with great diligence to hide the treasure found in the field, could nevertheless not so conceal it as that some should not behold the stigmata in his hands and feet . . . While he yet lived, many brethren saw them . . . At the time of his death, more than fifty brethren beheld them, as did Clare, that virgin most devoted unto God, with the rest of her sisters, and countless seculars. . . ." *

The hour of San Damiano had reached its culmination.

*Life of St. Francis, trans. E. Gurney Slater (N.Y.: Dutton, 1951), pp. 507-512.

COMMUNITY:
The History of an Experience

I

Is it not true that for everyone who participated actively and intelligently in the life of the past few decades the word "community" embraces an entire history—a history of profound experiences both pleasant and unpleasant, of fulfillment and disappointment at the same time?

This essay is an attempt to explain that history, which has been verified in the lives of many. Wisdom should be gained from it, so that the value of the experience is not lost—lost in the resignation with which the man who has acquired prudence looks back to the dreams and idealism of youth when reality was still a stranger.

Something is presupposed here: the experience of that history; that strong tendency toward community; the gamble in the belief that community was possible, that it really opened the doors of the ego, that the "we" was not only spoken but actually lived. Should this experience with all its nobility and its foolishness be wanting, then the following exposition will be nothing more than a presentation of cold, arid wisdom. But surely we are not speaking of anything like that. Perhaps an attempt ought to be made to re-establish that faith, which possibly went awry, on a higher level. To attain that plane, however, the experience must first be admitted, lived through, and matured as to the core of its meaning.

Life has a number of levels in its construction and progress. It cannot be known by a single, uniform act of judgment, but only through several contrary ones, that is, in terms of tension. Life simply cannot be lived as movement in one direction. Hence the apparent contradictions in the life of a genuinely vital person. The same holds true of the experience of community when we consider it as a history.

Initially, the movement of life was directed toward the

community—simply, immediately. Then came the experience of which we shall say more. Life took the opposite course, oriented toward solitude, again simply and entirely one-sidedly, perhaps with a feeling of bitter disappointment.

Neither of these two movements is right. That is to say, both are right, but neither entirely and solely by itself. If both are correctly developed, life as a whole achieves a new level. Then it appears not in a purely simple fashion, but with a tension of its own. Community and solitude determine one another mutually, for both are directed to the spiritual person.

II

When we spoke of "community," when we rapturously discovered that timorous and self-seeking individualism could be overcome, and that community was possible, what did we mean? By "we"—I mean our age, those persons in whom the heart of this age beat and who followed its impulse. When there was talk of community between man and man; of the possibility of question and response; of the power of being united; of the community of the nation as a living unity in destiny, work, responsibility and honor; when we spoke of the community of nations among themselves in the unity of the human mission on this progressively shrinking earth—what was meant by all that?

Certainly this: that man cannot be a recluse immured in himself, but that doors stand open and roads lead from one man to another; that the other person can be viewed and understood as he is; that he can be addressed and he in turn can address; that there is word and counter-word, utterable and intelligible; that it is possible to cooperate in perfecting another's life and to see one's own perfected by him; that there is a wondrous sharing in giving and receiving, in sorrow and in joy, in goods and values, in duties and destinies, in events, wisdom and deep feelings; in fact, that there are powers, streams of energy, inter-relations of events, similarity of form, which exist intimately in the other person and in myself simultaneously, which embrace both of us, with the result that I am simply in the other and he in me.

This occurrence was like a building of walls, like a bridging of an intervening chasm. The goals toward which different individuals lifted their eyes became sublimated in great unities. The roots from which various forms of life sprang showed themselves interwined, and there arose con-sciousness of a soil that nourished them all.

The man who has really experienced this, and as a result has not only thought and spoken, but acted and met destiny; in him, it appears to me, a history has been accomplished.

III

What about this man whose community we shall treat?

With many aspects of his being he exists simply in nature. He breathes and eats and drinks; he uses his senses; in him a world of passions is in ferment. All this happens in the first man, in the one beside him, in the third and in all. When I look at another, I see all this in him, understand it without difficulty, experience it with him. That the other man takes food when he is hungry; that his lungs inhale air so that his blood may be purified; all that and much else is self-evident, common to him and to me.

Without further consideration, we have in common the desire for earthly possessions, for things that ease, assure and fulfill life. Common is the longing of the blood. Common the longing for some kind of recognition, acceptance.

Common, too, are the basic forms of thought: the sense of cause and effect, of expression and of the matter to be expressed, of the manifold relations of things. Common are the basic forms of cultural existence and creativeness, the ultimate structures and values of economics, of politics, of art.

Individual existence does not arise spontaneously; it proceeds from the life of the parents. It develops from the material conditions, from the powers and formative aspects of the family. It is borne along, fostered, determined by the environments of school, society, and the age. All this spells immediate communality, and presents itself as such to consciousness. If one man considers other men, his vital act of thinking contains the same substance, which is drawn from the environment, as exists in them. And what he thinks affects the pulse of his heart, the structure of his being, the progress of his spiritual life.

Indeed, we can attempt to pursue the question to its ultimate end: do self-sufficient individuals really exist? Do I ever find myself in a position where I am absolutely alone? I think not. This becomes evident particularly with reference to one point: all thinking, no matter how intimate, hidden and "spiritual," eventuates in the word. We think in the form of interior speech. But all speech presupposes a listener. By nature we engage in dialogue.

A story is told of the Hohenstaufen Frederic II. At one time the question arose in his court of the original language of mankind, whether—as the matter was viewed in that epoch—it was Hebrew or Latin. Allegedly the emperor had a number of children brought together. He supplied them with living accommodations and all necessary services, but strictly forbade the nurses to speak the least word to their charges. The result was that the children did not begin to speak Hebrew, nor did they speak Latin, but—they died.

Speech is not something added to a complete human existence. We exist in the word, in conversation, hence in relation
to others and by the universal communality of life. No
doubt the same thing could be shown with regard to all the
basic acts of our existence.

We simply cannot avoid involvement. But if we thoroughly consider the situation, we feel that everywhere
differences arise.

One nation differs from another. Each embraces a common fund of similar basic sentiments and ideas, similar ways
in which men meet the world and move about in it. It is
precisely these things that differentiate one people from
another. When the German speaks confidently of "culture,"
this term represents for him elements that he regards with
almost religious reverence. The same thought translated into
French would appear singular, pedantic or stilted. For the
German, culture is service to the ultimate verities; for the
Frenchman, on the other hand, it is the form that makes a
man a man, the manner in which one man behaves toward
another. It is "civilization"—a continuation of the ancient
urbanitas, a noble existence replete with all values, beneficent toward others. German "culture" has a metaphysical
and cosmic character; the French counterpart, "civilization,"
possesses a human and above all a social character. As soon
as we say "society," we immediately sense that it has less
serious significance in the German world of thought, while
in truth it is a notion that is most profound and full of
precious values. Within the national and cultural communities further groups may be distinguished: tribal entities,
cities, families. These, too, by themselves form communities,
so that within them one man immediately knows what
another is about if he takes a position regarding a thing.
But each community in its turn erects barriers to unrelated

groups. If someone tries to establish a cooperative project throughout the German people, he will discover the barriers existing between a Swabian and a Rhinelander or between a Saxon and a Westphalian. Everyone has experienced in daily life how definitely one family with its peculiar nature and traditions differs from another, or what difficulties must be overcome when some eventuality brings people out of their social circle into another.

This fact emphasizes that phenomenon which plays so great a role in modern psychology: the basic structure of every man. It demonstrates that a man's peculiarities, rather than being heaped together helter-skelter, are grouped in constant forms: types, characters, temperaments or whatever they may be called. These determine manners of thinking, of taking positions regarding people and things, of feeling, of acting, of forming one's environment. In a word, they regulate matters of choice concerning determined values and basic concepts of reality.

There is, for example, the type who regards his fellow-man trustfully. With everyone he finds similarities and peaceful relationships; existence seems to smile on him, to be permeated by a beneficent order. But there is another type who by disposition sees chasms opening everywhere, who senses contradictions, inadequacies and opposition. For him existence resolves itself into a series of irreconcilable decisions. Again and again he feels drawn to combat. Insoluble problems and contradictions prevent him from generating confidence and keep him in an attitude of defense and caution. The most varied personality types can be defined in this way: inventive and conformist, constructive and historical, individual and social, those of varying breadth, of varying depth, and so on. Two individuals who share similarity of being will readily discover a common ground.

But between such as belong to different types, a barrier already exists.

Still, these various types do not exist in a pure form. Different aspects are united in one and the same person. True, one will always predominate and determine an individual's character; but it will be crisscrossed, colored, toned down by others. Thus, even within the purview of the same typical confines, man again differs from man, for the qualitatively and quantitatively varied forms of complexity will scarcely overlap.

As a result, the existential image tends to shrink—until it reaches those peculiar qualities which this individual alone possesses.

But a person is individualized not only by what he is, that is, by his essential form, but also by what he has experienced, by the form destiny has given him. The latter will include the environment in which he matured, and the character of his parents and family, teachers, friends and adversaries. This complex of forms enters into his living fiber, into the plastic memory of his body and disposition. He lives by the persons who have penetrated into his life and determined it. This form of destiny will include what he has done and what has been done to him. An action performed by him does not vanish; it continues to live in him. Every word leaves its mark in his living being. Every event, every experience, be it pleasant or ugly, constructive or destructive, leaves its trace. Thus at every moment man lives by the heritage of what went before. If, then, one man is compared with another, the whole of his life stands behind him, and that holds true of every man. To what extent do they have things in common?

This is the situation of our living being: I possess wide areas in common with all men. Then there are more restricted fields. Fewer agree with me in these. The zones always shrink, always the areas I share with others grow smaller, until finally I am in a closed circle drawn about myself alone. And it is an event, a gift, and, at the same time, a gamble, if these areas open out to another, if one man can be united with another in them.

But when I get to my innermost being, is there really a possibility of sharing? In the realm where I am face to face with myself, where I know myself most perfectly—is sharing possible there? When I recognize and acknowledge the inevitable, "thus I am—I am this person—this has been allotted me," and accept my self and my destiny; when in a moral decision I assume responsibility for my being and my actions—is that not essential solitude, concerned solely with my own self, particularly when I stand before God? Every soul is a special creation of God. Each is unique. In creating him, God calls every man in the individuality of his person; he calls him by his "name"—a name known only to God and to the person. It expresses what God intends him to be; it is the gift of God and, at the same time, his demand. The name represents the yardstick by which God will measure him, and the form of God's love for him. This ultimate personality exists only in the spiritual relationship of the child of God to the Creator. Here is definitive solitude. God's providence and the soul's modesty enshroud the mystery. But from this solitary center the ultimate determination permeates everything. To the extent that a person truly becomes a Christian, a child of God, to that same extent his entire existence is determined by that fact. To the same degree the person becomes a solitary figure, no matter how much he may be engaged in everyday life. His innermost being is veiled, because it stands before God. It becomes inaccessible, impenetrable, unattainable.

But what of the community if all this is true?

IV

It seems to me that the man who has dared to deal with the community sincerely has undergone a definite experience.

He really attempted to acquire communality. He was convinced that men are brothers. To be a "brother" implies not wanting to have anything in which another would not share. Distinction here becomes injustice; reservation becomes theft. All doors must stand open. Convictions must be common, as must values and goals. Work must be companionship; joy, a giving and a receiving; assistance, a matter of course.

He has really tried to put this into practice, and the more sincere he was in the attempt, the more clearly he sees that such communality can be very disturbing. True, doors must stand open; but they must also be closed. Largess becomes impossible if no reserve remains. Sharing is possible only if something actually exists that can be shared. Giving and receiving presuppose prudence, discretion. People are different; they vary in dignity and power. Every gift should find its place with the right person, otherwise it is not a gift, but waste. What helps one man may destroy another. What one man regards as precious, another looks upon as trash. Many a young family for this reason has not achieved its rightful form, calm and security, but is overwhelmed, drawn into the publicity of ceaseless give and take. Many an incipient work has not reached fruition, because the community made too many demands. Many a man has not acquired a mature character, because regularly that which demanded the strong reply of the responsible "I" was absorbed into the formless "we."

To the degree that he was conscious of all this, he began to doubt the possibility of abiding by the community.

He became aware that to a great extent community is

taboo. It must be excluded to safeguard one's own being; to preserve peace in one's home; to maintain independence of action, with its sense of freedom and responsibility; to preserve the sphere that to him is sacred and delicate, his liberty and his mystery. For the sake of his neighbor, too, community may not be admitted, lest he be deprived of what is his own, lest he be burdened with what does not pertain to him, lest it bring confusion into his being.

In fact, he had to acknowledge this: in many things I cannot have community, even should I attempt it. Much cannot be transferred to it, cannot be detached; it adheres to me. And my neighbor cannot receive it, assimilate it into his being, even should he wish to do so, because it has not been allotted to him. It simply does not pass over into the texture, the measure of his being.

Thus arose the first crisis—"first," though not in time, for everything we are saying should be envisaged not so much as a history in time, but as a history in meaning: the idea of community seemed to be called into question, and yet at the same time it could not be abandoned.

The outcome was this: if such community cannot offer immediate sharing of one with another, if in the final analysis everyone is inextricably attached to what is his own; we shall at least try to understand one another. Community then implies contemplating the other person in his being in order to know him better. I cannot be that other person. He must be himself. But I intend to understand him, and thereby to be united with him. He must go his way; I must go mine. But I shall pursue my way in such a manner that he will go on that side and I on this, so that thus we may become one in mutual understanding. He must perform his action and I mine. But I shall observe how it proceeds from him, how he intends it, how he lives in his action, because it is so intimately his. In like manner he will know me. Thereby we shall exercise communality. The knowledge of the one will protect and support the other. As a result he will feel secure, recognized, that he is sharing responsibility. This understanding must then furnish the basis for confidence: I know as much about him as I know about myself; I know on what I am building when I build on him. On this understanding will also rest fidelity: I know him as a clearly seen foundation; he will bear the house securely. Finally, this understanding will beget respect: I know that his being is genuine and deserves the accolade of esteem.

But then another crisis arose—the second and more profound crisis of community: Can I truly understand the next man? Yes, within the circles of existence that embrace both him and me. Can I pass beyond the limits of those circles? I know from experience that he does not understand a word which appears entirely obvious to me; that I misinterpret an action whose meaning, as later conversation reveals to me, was really quite clear. I notice that an action, proceeding from me and running its course within the field of my existence, has a definite significance; but as soon as it penetrates into that of another, it changes. In my world of experience a thing has a different meaning than in his. A mutually experienced event assumes a form in his spirit and consequent activity entirely different from the form it assumes in mine. I discover that where I thought I had understood another in his own being, I had in fact fashioned his image according to mine. Where I thought I had penetrated motives, I had actually misinterpreted them. I simplified the other person, I changed him, even changed him radically; possibly I did so repeatedly, in accord with the needs of the moment. I understood a definite stratum of his personality, but not what lay beneath it. For a while I interpreted his action correctly, but I did not know from what depth it came, and that it had an entirely different weight.

I began to comprehend how often I was wrong; how foolish my judgments concerning the other person often were. I became conscious of how strange we were to one another, and still we believed ourselves united in knowledge and understanding.

Relations with people are initially borne along by the impulse of the individual's own zest for life. Life seeks confirmation in another person, to permeate him and by this penetration to duplicate itself in the other's life. In this process the image of the other person is reformed, superimposed, often completely changed. The fact that what was called understanding turned out in reality to be self-appraisal goes unnoticed. To the extent that the power of the impulse diminishes, the intensity of a friendship wanes, the freshness of an experience withers; to the extent that life as a whole cools off and loses its ardor to continually promote reality and transform it according to one's own will— to that same extent a strangeness arises between us. Thereupon follows the feeling of aloneness with its coldness, its despair, its skeptism and self-seeking. Then comes the decisive test.

I have come to realize that the community of sharing is possible only within definite limits and that we must then appeal to community of understanding. But I have to admit also that this community of understanding is circumscribed, closely circumscribed. Now it depends on whether I realize that community, strictly speaking, has its decisive point in my recognizing the other person not only in his self-evident unique character, but also in his "otherness," in my acknowledging that perhaps in the last analysis the other person cannot really be known. Possibly all human relationships proceed from the unknown to the unknown.

Is it not true that I do not possess even my own self completely? That I am in the process of self-attainment?

That repeatedly the real self escapes me? The happiness I now enjoy, the task that I accomplish—is it not true that I do not really "have" it, but must struggle to grasp it, and that I never fully succeed? Thus the curious situation develops that I have done something—I and no one else—and yet my act somehow lies outside my firm possession; that entire strata of my being remain unpossessed by me. Possibly, as faith seems to say, only in the measure that I gain God shall I receive myself from his hand. If that is so, how much less can I claim to have a share in another? Then genuine communality demands that I renounce the impossible.

And is it not a fact that I do not understand my own self? That in the realm of my consciousness ideas emerge and again disappear like comets that rush in and out of the earth's atmosphere, and I do not know whence they come? Did not Paul say that he refused to judge himself, that he did not know whether he was really good or evil, that he left all judgment to God's tribunal? If that is so, then how shall I understand the other person? This I must consequently recognize and acknowledge. Accordingly, in the final analysis a possible communality means that I must acknowledge the other person despite the strangeness that separates us; that I must give him the freedom of his own being, which at the same time implies that I must respect his mystery and impenetrability; and that I, once I have promised him my fidelity, must observe it and have confidence in him, despite the strangeness.

Basic understanding does not demand penetration, but understanding is creative. It precedes and surpasses penetration. Confidence does not rest on penetration, but on itself; it proceeds from itself, repeatedly proceeds from itself. Confidence contains an element of chance. Fidelity does not find its basis in penetration. Fidelity creates its own basis.

V

Is this the end?

We ought to remind ourselves that a history is being recounted here—the history of a vital experience. That experience already faced an ending, namely, when the person took a chance with the community and realized where radical communality leads. That might have been the end, being lost in this radical community.

For such a situation exists. All of us are acquainted with the picture of a man who has been swallowed up in the "we"—perhaps even in the "it,"—the picture of a man who is always ready to let others be his conscience and to be, himself, the conscience of others, who consequently never abides in the solitude of genuine responsibility. He feels the continual urge to communicate himself and even to filch from the souls of others. He can never settle down; and in the perpetual flight from his own shortcomings, he throws himself into the education or care of others. And thus it goes on till we reach the man who can stay above water only through busyness and violent activity; he can bear neither solitude nor quiet, because they bring him face to face with reality. Here indeed we reach an end.

We assumed, however, that the man about whom we are speaking had seen these dangers, that his eyes had been opened, that he had looked about himself and had set out in the opposite direction. We tried to describe the stages of the new road.

But precisely on this path he seems to have run into another wall—from his confusion he passes into stark aloneness. The fact that he has tried to understand his neighbor and repeatedly failed can bring him to the point of despairing of the possibility of understanding or of being understood. It can lead him to consider his fellowman like the prisoner of Anatole France, whose dungeon opened to the sky only through very narrow slits; he saw the shadows of the passersby on the ceiling, but no living sound penetrated to him and none escaped. He wanted to do his share, but the opportunity did not present itself. He wanted to participate, but did not succeed. All this may lead him to the conclusion that every man has to fend for himself.

To justify his conclusion, he may create a philosophy. That can readily be done when the emotion of a disappointed heart governs reason. But the frigid quality of the lonely figure can be discerned.

VI

We are of the opinion, however, that the story does not end even here, but that it continues.

The person of whom we are speaking ought to appear startled and ask himself, "How can that be? Have I not twice already reached the limits of human endeavor? Twice gone to the very edge of the impossible, and in opposite directions? What does it all mean?"

It signifies the challenge to gain everything, the whole of human existence.

It would be wrong to look upon this as a challenge to moderation, that is, to exercise understanding, but to remain conscious of its limits; to practice communality, but to make reservations; to preserve solitude without losing relationships, and so on. That would be the famous "golden mean," and in truth something very cheap. Something more profound is meant, namely, the attainment of human wholeness, but on a different level.

The point is that man exists in nature and in the world, but always as a personal being.

Man stands in relationship to his species. But every

individual represents something unique, something that cannot be copied. Every man exists only once, uniquely. Not because it would be impossible to multiply him, but because, as a person possessed by himself, he is fundamentally unique.

The essence of every man is subject to the laws of nature and comprehensible by the laws of reason. But each man recognizes himself. By the fact that he thus knows about himself, a chasm opens beneath everything that can be known about him from outside—a chasm to which no direct path descends.

Every man is subject to "why" and "wherefore," but in the fact that he freely decides by himself lies an insoluble problem for the sharpest intellect and a barrier to all disposition regarding him.

Every man with his living essence has his place in the forms, the types, and structures of human existence. But in the fact that he can say "I" lies the most profound possibility of his turning toward others a countenance which, absolutely speaking, cannot be grasped.

All this means that objects can be grasped, taken hold of, appropriated, controlled, simply and absolutely, by immediate apprehension; not so the person. No path leads immediately to the person. A barrier stands in the way.

Thus we are faced with the problem of the person. I grasp the person, enter into community with him, not by the simple act that signifies "that thing," but by the dialectical act that says "you."

It is in that act that one ego moves toward another. He takes his eyes off himself and looks to the other. He goes to meet that other, opens himself to the other. Thus that other ego, if he responds to the movement, can perfect himself in the meeting with the first ego and comprehend himself in it —and by the same token open himself and make possible a mutual perfection. That is συμπαθεια, love in one of its many forms and degrees.

This meeting is spontaneous; it arises by itself, cannot be forced. Either it appears or it does not appear; therefore it is experienced as a gift, beneficent or disastrous. Can it be anticipated? I believe so. It would appear to reside most significantly in the renunciation of an objective attitude. What I mean may be expressed as follows:

If I meet a person and the "you" is to come about, first of all eye seeks eye. Thus the way is opened from the whence to the whither, and a definite direction is taken.

Then there follows a movement, at first one of regression. The attitude proper to the person is above all one of reserve. First a concession, "You over there—be yourself!"

Thereby the connection of immediacy is ruptured. Gone is the naïve self-complacency that says, "I am the center of the world. Everything else revolves around me. Everything has meaning only in relation to myself." The correct attitude toward the other person says, "He is a center also. All existing things constitute an environment for him as well."

We must beware of taking this point too lightly. To do more than talk about it, to put it into practice interiorly, is an arduous task. Things exist in my consciousness and emotions not by themselves alone, purely "objectively," but as they are evaluated by me and related to me; not as "the" world, but as "my" world. To sacrifice that, even if only in intention, is most difficult. It implies the abandonment of the idea that everything centers on me; the renunciation whose pure execution gives birth to that wisdom and holiness which begins in everyday existence. It implies the real admission, not only in thought, but also in deed, that another person has a genuine center, a personal origin and a personal goal, that there is a relationship of things, a "world," that passes from him to me and from me to him.

4

In place of the naïve conception of the world—ethically naïve, that is, since technically, psychologically, esthetically, scientifically, socially it can be highly developed, even over-refined—in place of all that, I say, comes the conception of the world as personal and ethical. In place of the mono-centric, egocentric structure of the world in which—as is often asserted with remarkable smugness—a single point exists, one's own self, with all things and happenings only supplying the environment, with everything illumined, explained and evaluated from that standpoint alone, and not only things, but people as well, who are looked upon not as persons but only as living entities, as individuals, as a matter of fact, also as "things"—in place of this world simplified by the selfishness of the individual there now comes a world that grows always more complicated. This world has a polycentric structure; forms a multiple system of personal "centers"; contains numerous criss-crossing "environments" with their particular meanings, values and teleologies. I am confronted with as many environments, with their claims upon me, as there are genuine "you's." As often as I enter into a real relationship with others, so often are the centers of the world multiplied and thereby com-plicated. If my movement is toward another, I go from world to world, from center to center. As a result, I must transpose thoughts, values, sentiments from the central position of my ego to the central position of another. To understand no longer means merely to grasp an existing object, but to reverse my customary point of view and to look upon the other in such a way that the whole world, all existence, centers in him.

What has been said is nothing more than the attempt to express clearly the true meaning of the following state-ments: "to love one's neighbor as oneself"; "not to do to another what one would not have done to oneself," and to indicate that great mysteries are involved here.

But the personal attitude signifies even more. It means that I cannot simply "possess" the thing outside me, but that I must by a continually renewed movement acquire it again and again.

If, in passing through the barrier of the centrality of the world, I have with my understanding attained the other person—I take for granted that I have reached him and really understood him—then I have now fully comprehended him. Still this comprehension cannot be stated in a hard and fast formula. If tomorrow the question arises not only of the comprehension of a psychological structure, but again of the understanding of the other person, then the movement must be repeated. This movement will be of varying force, determined by special circumstances, by the changing situations of the day. But by the fact that it is carried out at all, personal understanding results. Otherwise it is nothing but psychological knowledge—a recognition of happenings, an application of significant and orderly concepts, and so on. Personal understanding can be gained anew only by the repeated movement toward the other person. This is true not only because otherwise the other's movement is curbed and he is limited to a definite field—while all true relationship to another proclaims, "Be what you are; continue to grow, so that you may become what you ought to be"—but because personalized understanding is essentially possible only through the movement of approach and sight.

Even if I reached the other person in carrying out the movement and he gave himself to me in confidence, in love, in real sharing, still my possession would not be absolute ownership. Tomorrow I would not be able to boast, "Now I 'have' you," but I would have to carry out the movement anew, even though, and precisely when, fidelity survives and love remains alive. For love consists essentially in movement. It is not a frame, not a bridge built once for all, but a passing over and an existence in the "you." It exists *in fieri,* as the ancient philosophy puts it, in constant activity. As soon as this movement ceases a selfish purpose, a function, takes its place. The same is true of fidelity. It is not a rope that is tied, not a wall erected once for all, but it is life—a living, ever-new activity. Fidelity is a *habitus,* but one that must continually go over into action if it is to retain its personal character and not become a mere possession, as one might possess a thing. As soon as the latter happens, it is no longer fidelity but a state of ownership, not of a person but of a thing or a living entity. That is hardly a comfortable situation, particularly if the first sustaining emotion has subsided and the other person no longer directly attracts, but has become known, used to, "uninteresting"; if the completely known begins to irritate, his negative aspects appear more clearly, and so on. Then there is a call for genuine fidelity. Such fidelity can be very demanding and very strenuous; but only through it is true penetration to the personal accomplished.

Thus, from the twofold decision which was the subject of our discussion, a new creation comes about.

THE MEANING OF MELANCHOLY

Melancholy is too painful, it reaches too deeply into the roots of human existence to permit us to leave it to the psychiatrists.

If we inquire here into its meaning, that already implies that we are treating not a psychological or psychiatric situation, but a spiritual problem. We believe there is question here of something closely related to the depths of human nature.

In order to indicate what we are dealing with, we shall preface our remarks with some passages from the writings and journals of a man who himself probed the depths of melancholy. In him it was not only a power that colored his thought and action, an inner situation that gave tone to his entire existence; he went beyond all that and consciously took his melancholy upon himself as the starting point of his moral obligation, as the arena of his religious wrestling. I mean Sören Kierkegaard. The following passages are intended to delimit the area and to indicate clearly the inner dimensions in which this phenomenon, perhaps the most painful in human existence, moves.

"The terrible thing is when a man's consciousness is subjected to such pressure from childhood up that not even the elasticity of the soul, nor all the energy of freedom can rid him of it. Sorrow in life can certainly depress the conscious, but if the sorrow first appears at a mature age it does not have time to take that natural form, it becomes an historic fact, not something which lies as it were beyond the conscious itself. The man who has borne such a pressure from childhood up is like a child who has been taken from its mother with forceps and who always bears a memento of its mother's suffering."[1]

---

1. *The Journals of Sören Kierkegaard,* ed. and trans. Alexander Dru (N.Y.: Oxford University Press, 1938, 1959), p. 112.

"So I went forth into life, favored in every way, so far as intellectual gifts go and outward circumstances. Everything was done and continued to be done to develop my mind as richly as possible. Self-confident—yet with a decided sympathy or predilection for suffering, or for whatever in any way is suffering or oppressed. In a certain sense I may say that I went out into life with a proud and almost foolhardy bearing. I have never at any instant in my life been deserted by the faith that one can do what one will—only one thing excepted, all else unconditionally, but one thing not, the throwing off of the melancholy in whose power I was. What I am saying will seem to others a vain conceit, but so it was with me in truth, as truly as what I tell next, which to others again will seem a conceit. I say that it never remotely occurred to me that in my generation there lived or was to be born a man who had the upper hand of me—and in my inmost self I was the most wretched of all men. It never remotely occurred to me that, even if I were to attempt the most foolhardy enterprise, I should not be victorious—only one thing excepted, all else absolutely, but one thing not, the throwing off of the melancholy from which and from its attendant suffering I was never entirely free even for a day. This, however, must be understood in connexion with the fact that I was very early initiated into the thought that to conquer means to conquer in an infinite sense, which in a finite sense means to suffer. So this corresponded with my melancholy's inward apprehension that, in a finite sense, I was utterly good for nothing."[2]

"It seems to me as if I were a galley slave chained to death. Whenever life moves, the chain rattles, and death causes everything to wither—and this happens at every moment."[3]

2. *The Point of View for My Work as an Author,* trans. Walter Lowrie (N.Y.: Harper & Row, 1962), p. 78.

3. *Tagebücher,* answ. u. über von Th. Haecker (Innsbruck, 1923), I, 83.

"The terrible thing about the absolute spiritual incapacity from which I am suffering at the present time is that it is coupled with a consuming desire, with a spiritual passion,—and yet so formless that I do not even know what I long after."[4]

"The whole of existence frightens me, from the smallest fly to the mystery of the Incarnation; everything is unintelligible to me, most of all myself; the whole of existence is poisoned in my sight, particularly myself. Great is my sorrow and without bounds; no man knows it, only God in heaven, and he will not console me; no man can console me, only God in heaven, and he will not have mercy upon me. . . ."[5]

"I have just returned from a party of which I was the life and soul; wit poured from my lips, everyone laughed and admired me—but I went away—and the dash should be as long as the earth's orbit ——————————————
———————————— and wanted to shoot myself."[6]

"What reconciled me with my fate and with my sufferings was that I, the so unhappy, so much tortured prisoner, had obtained this unlimited freedom of being able to deceive, so that I was allowed to be absolutely alone with my pain. It goes without saying that this was quite enough to render all my other abilities anything but merry for me. When this is given (i.e. such a pain and such a close reserve), it depends upon the personal characteristics of the individual whether this lonesome inward torment finds its expression and satisfaction in hating men and cursing God, or in the very reverse. The latter was my situation. As far back as I can remember I was in agreement with myself about one thing, that for me there was no comfort or help to be looked for in

4. *The Journals*, p. 85.
5. *The Journals*, p. 72 f.
6. *The Journals*, p. 26 f.

others. Sated with many other things bestowed upon me, filled as a man with longing after death, as a spirit desirous of the longest possible life, my thought was, as the expression of a melancholy love for men, to be helpful to them, to find comfort for them, above all clearness of thinking, and that especially about Christianity. The thought goes very far back in my recollection that in every generation there are two or three who are sacrificed for the others, are led by frightful sufferings to discover what redounds to the good of others. So it was that in my melancholy I understood myself as singled out for such a fate."[7]

"For my misfortune (almost I might say from my birth, completed by my upbringing) was . . . not to be a man. But when one is a child—and the other children play or jest or whatever else they do; ah! and when one is a youth—and the other young people make love and dance or whatever else they do—and then, in spite of the fact that one is a child or a youth, then to be a spirit! Frightful torture! Even more frightful if one by the help of imagination knows how to perform the trick of appearing to be the youngest of all. But this misfortune is already diminished when one is forty years old, and in eternity it does not exist. I have never had any immediacy, and therefore, in the ordinary human sense of the word, I have never lived. I began at once with reflection; it is not as though in later years I had amassed a little reflection, but I am reflection from first to last. In the two ages of immediacy (childhood and youth) I, with the dexterity reflection always possesses, helped myself out, as I was compelled to do, by some sort of counterfeit, and not being quite clear myself about the talents bestowed upon me, I suffered the pain of not being like the others. . . ."[8]

"It is extraordinary how strictly, in a certain sense, I

7. *The Point of View*, p. 78 f.
8. *The Point of View*, p. 81.

was brought up. Sometimes I was put into the black hole,
there I creep around in an agony of pain, seeing nothing,
knowing no way out, then suddenly a thought would awaken
in my soul, as alive as though I had never known it before,
though it might not be unknown to me, but up till then I
had, as it were, only been married to it with my left hand,
and now with my right. When it had taken root in me, I
was caressed a little, was taken in its arms and I, who was
all shrivelled up like a grasshopper grow as healthy, well-
fed, happy, blood-warm, and limber as a new-born babe.
Then I have to give my word that I will follow this thought
to the very end, stake my life upon it, and then I am
harnessed to it. So I get to the end, and everything begins
again from the beginning."[9]

"The same thing has happened to me again that has
happened so often before. While I am submerged in the
deepest suffering of melancholy, some thought or other
becomes so knotted up that I cannot disentangle it, and
since it is connected with my own life I suffer incredibly.
And then after a certain time has gone by, the abscess bursts
—and underneath lies the richest and most beautiful
material for hard work and of the very kind I need at that
moment.

"But while the suffering lasts it is often horribly painful. Yet little by little, one learns with God's help to remain
faithfully with God even during the suffering, or at least to
return to God as quickly as possible when it seems as though
he had left one for a moment while one suffered. It must
be so, for if it were possible to remain quite close to God
while one suffered, one would not suffer at all."[10]

"I got up in the morning feeling uncommonly well. This
sense of well-being increased out of proportion to all analogy

9. *The Journals*, p. 117 f.
10. *The Journals*, p. 259.

during the forenoon. Precisely at one o'clock I was at the highest peak and surmised the dizzy maximum which is not indicated on any scale of well-being, not even on the poetical thermometer. The body had lost all its earthly heaviness, it was as though I had no body, just for the reason that every function enjoyed its completest satisfaction, every nerve tingled with delight on its own account and on account of the whole, while every pulsation, as a disquietude in the organism, only suggested and reported the sensuous delight of the instant. My gait became a glide, not like the flight of a bird that cleaves the air and leaves the earth behind, but like the billows of the wind over a field of grain, like the yearning bliss of the cradling waves of the sea, like the dreamy gliding of the clouds. My very being was transparent, like the depths of the sea, like the self-contented silence of the night, like the quiet monologue of midday. Every feeling of my soul composed itself to rest with melodious resonance. Every thought proffered itself freely, every thought proffered itself with festal gladness and solemnity, the silliest conceit no less than the richest idea. Every impression was surmised before it arrived and was awakened within me. The whole of existence seemed to be as it were in love with me, and everything vibrated in preordained *rapport* with my being. In me all was ominous, and everything was enigmatically transfigured in my microcosmic bliss, which was able to transform into its own likeness all things, even the observations which were most disagreeable and tiresome, even disgusting sights and the most fatal collisions. When precisely at one o'clock I was at the highest peak, where I surmised the ultimate attainment, something suddenly began to chafe one of my eyes, whether it was an eye-lash, a mote, a bit of dust, I do not know; but this I know, that in that selfsame instant I toppled down almost into the abyss of despair. . . ."[11]

11. *Repetition: an Essay in Experimental Psychology*, trans. Walter Lowrie (Princeton: Princeton University Press, 1961), p. 74 ff.

"*May 19. Half-past ten in the morning.* There is an indescribable joy which enkindles us as inexplicably as the apostle's outburst comes gratuitously: 'Rejoice I say unto you, and again I say unto you rejoice.'—Not a joy over this or that but the soul's mighty song 'with tongue and mouth, from the bottom of the heart': 'I rejoice through my joy, in, at, with, over, by, and with my joy'—a heavenly refrain, as it were, suddenly breaks off our song; a joy which cools and refreshes us like a breath of wind, a wave of air, from the trade wind which blows from the plains of Mamre to the everlasting habitations."[12]

"It is said of the 'poet' that he invokes the muse to supply him with thoughts. This indeed has never been my case, my individuality prohibits me even from understanding it; but on the contrary I have needed God every day to shield me from too great a wealth of thoughts. Give a person such a productive talent, and along with that such feeble health, and verily he will learn to pray. I have been able at any instant to perform this prodigy, and I can do it still: I could sit down and continue to write for a day and a night, and again for a day and a night; for there was wealth sufficient for it. If I had done it, I should have been broken. Oh, even the least dietetic indiscretion, and I am in mortal danger. When I learn obedience, as I have described above, when I do the work as if it were a sternly prescribed task, hold the pen as I ought, write each letter with pains, then I can do it. And thus, many and many a time, I have had more joy in the relation of obedience to God than in thoughts that I produced."[13]

"Thus it is that in the course of my whole activity as an author I have constantly needed God's aid so as to be able to do the work simply as a prescribed task to which

12. *The Journals,* p. 59.
13. *The Point of View,* p. 68.

definite hours every day were allotted, outside of which it was not permissible to work. And if only once that rule was transgressed, I had to pay for it dearly. Nothing is less like my procedure than the stormy entrance of genius upon the scene, and then its tumultuous *finale*. Substantially I have lived like a clerk in his *comptoir*. From the very beginning I have been as it were under arrest and every instant I have sensed the fact that it was not I that played the part of master, but that another was Master. I have sensed that fact with fear and trembling when he let me feel his omnipotence and my nothingness; have sensed it with indescribable bliss when I turned to him and did my work in unconditional obedience. The dialectical factor in this is that whatever extraordinary gift may have been entrusted to me, it was entrusted as a precautionary measure with such elasticity that, if I were not to obey, it would strike me dead. It is as if a father were to say to his child: You are allowed to take the whole thing, it is yours; but if you will not be obedient and use it as I wish—very well, I shall not punish you by taking it from you; no, take it as yours . . . it will smash you. Without God I am too strong for myself, and perhaps in the most agonizing of all ways am broken. Since I became an author I have never for a single day had the experience I hear others complain of, namely, a lack of thoughts or their failure to present themselves. If that were to happen to me, it would rather be an occasion for joy, that finally I had obtained a day that was really free. But many a time I have had the experience of being overwhelmed with riches, and every instant I bethought me with horror of the frightful torture of starving in the midst of abundance—if I do not instantly learn obedience, allow God to help me, and pro-duce in the same fashion, as quietly and placidly as one performs a prescribed task.

"But in still another sense I have needed God's aid, time

and again, day after day, year after year, in the whole course
of my activity as a writer. For he has been my one confidant,
and only in reliance upon his cognizance have I dared to
venture what I have ventured, and to endure what I have
endured, and have found bliss in the experience of being
literally alone in the whole vast world, alone because wher-
ever I was, whether in the presence of all, or in the presence
of a familiar friend, I was always clad in the costume of my
deceit; so that I was then as much alone as in the darkness
of the night; alone, not in the forests of America with their
terrors and perils, but alone in the company of the most
terrible *possibilities*, which transform even the most frightful
actuality into a refreshment and relief; alone, almost with
human speech against me; alone with torments which have
taught me more than one new annotation to the text about
the thorn in the flesh; alone with decisions in which one had
need of the support of friends, the whole race if possible;
alone in dialectical tensions which (without God) would
drive any man with my imagination to madness; alone in
anguish unto death; alone in the face of the meaninglessness
of existence, without being able, even if I would, to make
myself intelligible to a single soul—but what am I saying,
'to a single soul'?—nay, there were times when it could
not be said in the common phrase, '*that* alone was lacking,'
times when I could not make myself intelligible to myself.
When now I reflect that years were passed in this manner,
I shudder. When but for a single instant I see amiss, I sink
in deep waters. But when I see aright and find repose in the
assurance of God's cognizance, blessedness returns again."[14]

"Has a man the right to desire his own destruction? No!
Why not? Because then this longing either has its basis in a
loathing of life—in which case he ought to have the fortitude
to combat it, or the reason lies in the fact that he wants to

15. *Tagebücher*, II, p. 220.

be more than a man. True enough, there are instances in which human intelligence can see that here a sacrifice would produce a tremendous effect. But to desire his own destruction—that is too exalted for a man.

"To desire his destruction is so exalted that only the Divine can perfectly possess this desire. In every man who wants something of the kind there will always exist an admixture of melancholy. Perhaps it is a stifled wish or something akin to it about which he personally despairs (for with God all things are possible), and now his passion grasps at this kind of heroism.

"But this is not permissible. A man should express his desires before God, do what is humanly possible to fulfill them, ask God to do it—and then leave it to God whether possibly he ought to go toward his destruction in this way. In a word, a man ought to be a man."[15]

"From a child I was under the sway of a prodigious melancholy, the depth of which finds its only adequate measure in the equally prodigious dexterity I possessed of hiding it under an apparent gaiety and *joie de vivre*. So far back as I can barely remember, my one joy was that nobody could discover how unhappy I felt. This proportion (the equally great magnitude of melancholy and of the art of dissimulation) signifies that I was relegated to myself and to a relationship with God. As a child I was sternly and seriously brought up in Christianity. Humanly speaking, it was a crazy upbringing. Already in my earliest childhood I broke down under the grave impression which the melancholy old man who laid it upon me himself sank under. A child—what a crazy thing!—travestied as an old man! Frightful! What wonder then that there were times when Christianity appeared to me the most inhuman cruelty—although never, even when I was farthest from it, did I cease to revere

15. *Tagebücher,* II, p. 220.

it, with a firm determination that (especially if I did not myself make the choice of becoming a Christian) I would never
initiate anyone into the difficulties which I knew and which
so far as I have read and heard, no one else has alluded to.
But I have never definitely broken with Christianity nor
renounced it. To attack it has never been my thought. No,
from the time when there could be any question of the
employment of my powers, I was firmly determined to employ them all to defend Christianity, or in any case to present it in its true form. For very early indeed, by the help of
my upbringing, I was in a position to ascertain for myself
how seldom Christianity is presented in its true form, how
they who defend it most commonly betray it, and how
seldom its opponents really hit the mark—although, in my
opinion at least, they often squarely hit established Chris-
tendom, which might rather be called the caricature of true
Christianity, or a monstrous amount of misunderstanding,
illusion, etc., mixed with a sparing little dose of true Christianity. So I loved Christianity in a way: to me it was vener-
able—it had, to be sure, humanly speaking, rendered me
exceedingly unhappy. This corresponds to my relationship
with my father, the person whom I loved most deeply. And
what is the meaning of this? The point precisely is that he
made me unhappy—but out of love. His error did not consist
in lack of love, but in mistaking a child for an old man. To
love him who makes one happy, is to a reflective mind an
inadequate definition of what love is; to love him who made
one unhappy out of malice, is virtue; but to love him who
out of love, though by a misunderstanding, yet out of love,
made one unhappy—that is the formula never yet enun-
ciated, so far as I know, but nevertheless the normal formula
in reflection for what it is to love."[16]

"Marvellous how God's love overwhelms me! Ah, basi-

16. *The Point of View*, p. 76 f.

5

cally I know no truer prayer than again and again to pray
that God may suffer me, that he be not angry with me because I continuously thank him for having done and for
doing—yes, and doing—so indescribably more for me than
I had ever expected. Surrounded by contempt, day after
day plagued by people, a nonentity even to my nearest rela-
tives, I know of nothing else here at home or in my innermost being but to thank God; for I understand I cannot
describe what he has done for me. A man—and after all
what is a man in God's sight, a zero, less than a zero; and
now take a man, subject to the most depressing melancholy
from childhood, an object of fear to himself. Then God
helps so marvellously and grants what he has granted me!
Life was a burden to me, however much at times I understood all the fortunate situations; everything was bitter to
me because of the black spot that spoiled everything. God
looked with favor on such a life. In quiet solitude he per-
mitted me to weep before him, again and again to bemoan
my torment, blessedly consoled by the knowledge that he
cared for me—and thereby he gave this life of pain a meaning that almost overwhelmed me, he gave me joy and
strength and wisdom for all my duties, to make my entire
existence a pure expression of ideas.

"Now, too, I understand so clearly (another occasion to
rejoice in God, to thank him anew) that my life has a goal.
My life began without any preliminaries, with a monstrous melancholy, in earliest childhood already shaken to its
deepest foundation, a melancholy that for a time plunged
me into sin and dissipation, which yet, humanly speaking,
was more madness than guilt. My father's death worked an
essential change in me. I did not dare to believe that this
fundamental distress of my being could be alleviated. Thereupon I laid hold of the eternal, blessedly convinced that God
is love, even though I should go on suffering thus through-

out my life. But I have that blessed conviction. That is how
I regarded my life."[17]

From the foregoing texts we perceive the weight of the
matter with which we are dealing, the mighty extent of this
phenomenon, the inner plenitude of its potential.

In a spirit of empathy with this man's world of ideas—
but beyond that also to a consideration of the phenomenon
itself—we shall attempt to grasp the significance, that
is, some of the significance, which it has for man, for
the development of his activity and personal status. Our
approach will not be psychological and medical, but spiritual. And I believe—to anticipate the conclusions somewhat—that we must understand melancholy as an experience in which the critical point of our human condition in
general becomes clear.

II

We shall proceed with caution. It is our intention to go from
the exterior to the interior, without asserting that we shall
be able to exhaust the entire extent and content of the
subject.

We are speaking of melancholy. Etymologically the
word means "black bile;" it conveys the idea of heaviness of
spirit. It rests like a weight upon man and presses him down.
He almost collapses; the members and organs lose their elasticity; the senses, urges, concepts and ideas become languid;
the will grows flaccid; incentive, joy in work and desire
weaken.

By reason of this disposition an inner fetter binds everything that otherwise acts freely, that otherwise moves and
produces results. The firmness of decision, the power of clear
and sharp conception, the courageous facing of a situation—

17. *Tagebücher*, II, pp. 376-78.

all these turn turgid and indifferent. Man no longer can master his life. He lags behind in the pressing struggle. Events heap up around him, and he no longer sees his way clearly. He dawdles with a single task. Meanwhile his problem mounts before him like a mountain that cannot be scaled.

As the result of such an experience Nietzsche characterized the spirit of melancholy as a demon. Out of it grew his image of yearning for the person "who can dance." For such an individual feelings, enthusiasm, the power to rise and to fly appear as the supreme values.

Such a life is extremely vulnerable. This vulnerability does not stem essentially from a defective constitution or a lack of inner power—though this sort of thing may be a complicating factor—but from a sensibility of man's being as conditioned by the existing multiplicity of situations. In my opinion, simple people do not become melancholy. "Simplicity" in this connection does not imply lack of education or modest social conditions. A person may be highly educated, capable, play a role in varied economic affairs and rewarding activities, and still be simple in this sense. Complicated, on the other hand, signifies inner opposition, contrary tendencies of life, tension between motives, a crisscrossing of urges, contradictions in attitudes toward persons and things, in the claims of the world and one's own person, in the criteria used in judgment.

Such sensibility makes the person vulnerable by reason of the harshness of existence. The damage is done precisely by the things that cannot be avoided: universal suffering, the woes of the weak and the defenceless, the sufferings of animals, the dumb creatures. Basically, of course, the individual cannot change these things. They are inevitable. That is the situation, and so it will remain. And yet it proves an intolerable burden. The wretchedness of existence strikes wounds—the fact that so often it is ugly, and so very dull.

And the emptiness of it; one might almost say, the meta-physical emptiness. At this point melancholy teams up with tedium, and a particular kind of tedium, as certain persons experience it. Not that the individual abstains from serious work, that he goes idle. Tedium of this kind can color a very active life. It implies that the person seeks something, seeks it everywhere and passionately—something that he cannot find. With a painful incompetence he seeks that which in the truest sense can be called bourgeois, a compromise with the possible and a sense of well-being. Tedium looks for that. It tries to see things as it would like them to be, to find in them that significance, that earnestness, that ardor and power of fulfillment for which it longs. But it does not succeed. Things are finite. But all finiteness is a defect. And this defect is a disappointment for the heart that longs for the absolute. This disappointment spreads till it creates the feeling of a great void. Nothing worthwhile exists. Nothing merits a claim on one's attention.

Ethical deficiencies of others cause wounds. Deficiencies of standards particularly, of ideals of character. And, of course, the base, the ordinary, strikes especially deep wounds.

We have used the word "vulnerability," and in fact the accent falls on it. This word expresses the characteristic coloring of melancholic suffering, which is more than simple disgust or vexation or pain. These indeed can be agonizing and vehement, exciting to passionate resistance. They may, however, always contain something luminous that goads the assertive powers to a decisive defense. In melancholy, on the other hand, we find something different, proper to itself, which touches the nerves. The suffering it produces has a special subjective character, a special depth; it is something unprotected, exposed. Missing is the will to resist, so that the cause of the wound unites itself with an element in man's

interior being. This proximity of the pain—to which might
be added an obvious lack of proportion between what might
be called the normal pain-effect of the cause and its profound effect in the melancholy person—makes it clear that
we are dealing with something constitutive. Its proper element does not reside in external causes and impulses, but in
man's interior—a kind of attraction to anything that can
injure.

This may become so extreme that the melancholy person experiences pain from any and every happening, no
matter what its nature. Existence by and in itself becomes
a source of pain to him.

Such a person lacks self-confidence. He is convinced that
he is less than others, that he is nothing, that he knows
nothing. And this is not because he is insufficiently gifted or
has suffered failures. The conviction exists *a priori*; it cannot
even be conclusively overcome by successful undertakings.
On the other hand, every failure confirms the conviction
beyond all reasonable limits. Furthermore, it is precisely this
lack of self-confidence which occasions the failures. It makes
the person insecure, confuses and hinders decision and
action, and makes the person painfully sensitive to external
difficulties.

This lack of self-confidence makes itself felt particularly
in relations with others—in conversation, in social contacts,
in public affairs. Perhaps here a particularly sensitive need
of acceptance also plays an important role.

Curiously, such a person at the same time may be vain
or proud; he may seek acclaim or recognition. Possibly even
his thoughts and fantasies are filled with dreams in which he
sees himself honored, powerful, engaged in enterprises that
call forth admiration. Similarly, the vulnerability referred to
above does not prevent him from being extremely sensitive

to the abundance of meaning, the wealth of values and the beauty inherent in the world.

The fact that the melancholy person is under this pressure, that existence so easily wounds him, that his power of self-evaluation and self-assertion leaves so much to be desired—all this is for him something active that turns on him like an enemy. The new psychology has advanced the view that what we call "life" is not something univocal. Instead, it allegedly is governed by a pair of basic urges that are diametrically opposed to one another: the one, to exist, to assert self, to develop, to progress; the other, to destroy self, to perish. This analysis seems to be correct. Does not such a view offer the only solution for the enigmatic manner in which we act? If something threatens us, we defend ourselves. But we do not simply defend ourselves; the danger also evokes a reply from us. The threatening object may indeed inspire fear, but it also entices. In the face of danger, of death, we go on the defensive. At the same time, however, we feel curiously attracted, because something in us urges us on.

From this vantage point we catch a glimpse of the ultimate metaphysical synthesis: here is the impulse for something spiritual, for the "great renunciation" of self, for the will to die in order that something more noble may arise.

All this ought to create a vital tension. Melancholy, however, tends to go off the deep end. The urge to self-destruction threatens to gain mastery. Pain and death become dangerously attractive. There is a violent temptation to let go of oneself.

Indeed, this will becomes active and turns upon the individual's own life. The urge to self-torture is connected with a melancholy disposition.

In the selection of an environment with powers of wounding we already perceive a subconscious desire.

This desire works by way of suggestion: the person considers himself sick, and thus he creates sickness for himself.

It manifests itself in self-induced distress of soul. Every thing available serves this end—everything, even the noblest, which by nature ought to elevate and fulfill. Here we touch the most muddled element of human existence: even values can become instruments of pain. A "value" signifies something that is worthy of existence; it is justified in being; it is precious, noble, exalted. "Value" expresses the fact that something is positive, capable of fulfilling a person, that it elevates, is meaningful. As soon as we contemplate a value in itself, for example the good, the just, the beautiful, it shows itself unequivocally as worthwhile, beneficent. But as soon as this value appears in real life, is experienced by real persons, carried out in practice, its effect can be multiple: to elevate, to fulfill, and at the same time to threaten, to cause anxiety. If we abstract from God, who is Good personified, we find a sure, unidirectional basis of action only in the realm of the pure idea, pure thought—and that solely in the field of pure nature with its regulated course. But if the value exists in the life of a person, borne along by the multiplicity of his inner powers, subject to his free desires, then the execution of something univocal can take on various forms. The more exalted the value, the more numerous the possibilities of its execution. The more exalted the value, the greater the possibility of its producing disturbing effects. It is wrong to conclude from the dangerous effect produced by a worthwhile value that it is counterfeit. Paradoxically, the most exalted values are the most dangerous. The great prizes are never won by a simple manner of life. They are paid for with the coin of anxiety and danger.

In the field of melancholy, a movement contrary to action makes itself strongly felt. The melancholy nature is conscious of values to a high degree. But the self-destructive tendency in it employs the value as the most dangerous weapon against itself. I think, for example, of the feeling of inferiority—an inferiority not at all justified—experienced by many artistic natures with regard to their own creations. The value of achievement, in itself very exalted, here becomes a disturbing factor. Or the inner impossibility experienced by many social types in facing the demands of justice; *a priori* the social value is so conceived that there is no prospect of its being realized, and for that reason it depresses. I think of the frightful destruction that can proceed from the two values, moral and religious, which determine the person's inner destiny; it is difficult to picture anything sadder than the profound confusion of a melancholy conscience. For its every duty becomes an intolerable burden; the desire for purity and perfection takes on an impossible form, unrelated to actual powers and circumstances. This conscience sees guilt where for everyone else there is none; it perceives responsibility where all its prerequisites are wanting. It sees moral criteria where only natural processes are involved. Possibly the threat posed by religious values can go even deeper. Dedication to what is holy, the desire to receive the divine into one's life, the striving to realize God's kingdom—all these impulses ought ordinarily to produce a liberative, expansive, elevating influence. In the case of the melancholy person, however, they can induce all sorts of fears and despair, driving him to the limits of fanaticism or to the delusion that he is lost or to revolt against what is holy. It seems as if a hidden will to destroy turns these highest of all values against the person's life, deprives them of positive meaning and brings to the fore only what is disturbing and threatening.[18]

18. What has been said does not mean to imply that the value as such disturbs or endangers; rather, because of the weakness of fallen man, the value tends to manifest itself in an ambivalent manner.

Here we are faced with the enigma of melancholy: life turns against itself, the instincts of self-preservation, self-respect, self-advancement are curiously confused, weakened, uprooted by the tendency toward self-destruction. It is not far wrong to assert that in melancholy destruction looms as a positive value, as something longed for and desirable. There is a manifest tendency to wish to suppress the possibility of one's existence, to knock away the sustaining props, to question the values that justify one's life—and thus to fall into a mental attitude which no longer sees any reason for living, which gads about in a senseless void, in despair.

Psychoanalysis attempted to trace this entire situation to sexual roots. Without discussing its meaningless exaggerations and generalizations, which create a picture of reality that is not only joyless but uninteresting, we can say that it is partially correct. The profound instinctive drives, which might be called the organic character of the manifestations, point in that direction. But the psychoanalytical explanation affects only certain strata of the problem. The real roots lie in the spiritual realm. We shall say more of that later. Indeed, at certain moments the attitude toward the self assumes a form which makes it difficult to exclude entirely the idea of the diabolical; for example, when the melancholy person literally and with all the fibers of his being hates himself. No matter how well the psychological mechanisms are analyzed and understood, at times the question formally arises: what really causes life to turn against itself? All of this begets a fear of people and drives the melancholy person to concealment and solitude.

Man's inner self, capable of being wounded, strives to stay out of the way of the element that can injure, for his own sake as well as—and this is an important point in the psychology of the melancholy person, who often has profound altruistic tendencies—for the sake of not wounding others. For every pain he causes falls back on himself with redoubled strength. This individual, so lacking in self-confidence, avoids being seen by others or addressed by them since he fears they may penetrate his misery. But the urge really arises from something more profound. It is the desire to plunge into the deep. This strong impulse for concealment shows itself in the avoidance of people. The melancholy person feels comfortable only when he is alone. No one needs quiet so much as he; to him this condition takes on the quality of a substance, a spiritual atmosphere that allows him to breathe freely, that soothes and hides. In the first pages of *Stages on Life's Way*, Kierkegaard speaks of quiet and solitude. They belong to the finest lines he has written.

"In Gribs-Forest there is a place called the Nook of Eight Paths; he alone finds it who worthily seeks it, for it is not indicated upon any map. The very name seems to involve a contradiction. For how can the junction of eight paths constitute a nook? How can that which implies travel in all directions accord with what is lonely and concealed? And what the solitary man shuns is named after the junction of only three paths: triviality—how trivial then must be the junction of eight paths! And yet it is so: there actually are eight paths, but very solitary paths. Though it is apparently remote, hidden and lonely, one is quite near the hedge of the enclosure, which is called Hedge of Ill Luck. So the contradiction in the name merely makes the place more solitary, as contradiction always does. The eight paths, the much traffic, are merely a possibility, a possibility for thought, since no one frequents these paths except a tiny insect which hurries across them *lente festinans*; no one frequents them except that cursory traveller who is continually looking about him on all sides, not in search of anyone but with the aim of avoiding everyone, that fugitive whom only the death-dealing bullet overtakes—which explains indeed why the stag now is still, but not why it was so restless; no one frequents them except the wind, of which no man knows whence it cometh or whither it goeth. Even the man who lets himself be deceived by the beguiling suggestion wherewith morbid reserve seeks to capture the wayfarer, even he who follows the narrow footpath which entices one into the recesses of the forest—even he is not so solitary as one on the eight paths along which no one travels! It is in fact as if the world were extinct and the survivor confronted by the embarrassment of having no one to bury him; or as if the whole tribe had wandered away by the eight paths and left one of the members behind—if it is true as the poet says, *bene vixit qui bene latuit,* then I have lived well, for my nook was well chosen. Certain it is too that the world and all that therein is never appears to better advantage than when it is seen from a nook and one must take a look at it by stealth; certain it is too that all one hears in the world or is able to hear sounds most enchanting and delicious when heard from a nook where one gives ear to it by stealth. So I often have resorted to my retired nook. I knew it before, long before, but now I have learned not to need the night in order to find quiet, for here it always is quiet, always beautiful, but most beautiful, as it seems to me, now when the harvest sun holds a vesper service, and the sky turns a languishing blue; when the creatures take breath after the heat, when coolness is released, and the leaves of the meadow shiver voluptuously, while the forest rustles; when the sun thinks of the evening when it will cool itself in the ocean, when the earth prepares itself for repose and thinks of thanksgiving, when before their parting the two come to an understanding with one another in the tender fusion which darkens the forest and makes brighter the green of the meadows.

"O friendly spirit which inhabitest these places, thanks be to thee for always protecting my quietness, thanks for those hours passed in serious recollection, thanks for thy hiding place which I call mine! There quietness increases as the shadows lengthen, as the silence grows—what a formula of enchantment to conjure with! How inebriating is quietness! For hastily as the drinker may raise the cup to his lips, his inebriation does not increase so rapidly as that of quietness, which grows every second! And what is the mere drop contained in the intoxicating cup in comparison with the infinite sea of silence from which I drink! And what is the seething of wine in contrast with the spontaneous ebullition which seethes more and more powerfully! But also what vanishes so quickly as this inebriation, if someone is merely heard to speak! And what more vexatious than the situation when suddenly one is wrested out of it—worse than the awakening of the drunkard it is when in silence one has forgotten speech, become shy at the sound of words!..."[19]

Such words could only be inspired by the yearning for quiet of a melancholy person.

His constant flight into concealment finds expression in the entire structure of his existence. It is an existence full of façades and masks. Again and again the extraneous hides what is proper to the person. Social forms, elegant idleness, wit, objective earnestness—all these are but a front behind which something quite different lurks—often dark despair.

In such circumstances self-revelation becomes difficult. It becomes well-nigh impossible to express simply what one thinks, the internal processes, to call the inner movements by their simple names. They are too heavily overladen with the unusual. They are of such a nature that others seemingly cannot grasp them. To the one who experiences them they

19. *Stages on Life's Way,* trans. Walter Lowrie (Princeton: Princeton University Press, 1945), pp. 33-35.

are horrible, unheard of, strange, fearful, perhaps ugly, and they certainly have no place in the workaday world.

The problem of expression mounts, as well as the differentiation between the external and the internal. For the melancholy person the internal experience and its external expression are incommensurable: spirit and body; intention and action; disposition and result; the beginning of a process and its completion. In general, the higher and the lower, the genuine and the false, the principal and the accessory are dualities between which the melancholy person sees a high wall erected. This difficulty of expression becomes very tragic, since the means of expression serve to hide what they were meant to reveal.

This tragic element can take on terrible proportions. Kierkegaard has possibly spoken the definitive word regarding this aspect of melancholy; his expressions rank with those of Dostoyevski. This is true above all of *The Concept of Fear,* in which he describes the diabolical. He characterizes it as fear of the good, a fear that arises when man has become immersed in evil. If the man in question is of a melancholy disposition such fear turns to extreme reserve. He dreads any disclosure of self, any glance others might direct into his being. This is true not only because he dreads the consequences of exposure, which would be a sign of a bad conscience, but because he shrinks from the good as such.

The beginning of all good is the "revelation" with which man sets himself in the light; the process of manifestation by profession. Here melancholy turns into that terrible state of reticence into which man draws himself in his rejection of the good. It is not profitable to speak overly much of these things, particularly not in our day when, side by side with the deep suffering of individuals, we find the brazenness of public prattling. Our writers speak much and gladly of the diabolical. The practice is fashionable. But those who speak thus know nothing of the diabolical. Abstracting from the fact that such persons abuse words, there exists the real danger that their lucubrations may fall into the soul of someone better than themselves—an earnest, suffering individual who says nothing but must bear his burden.

III

Hitherto we have spoken of the ponderousness of melancholy, of its negative character, of the suffering and the disturbances it causes. But something wonderful has shone through as well. Everywhere we have noted that precious, exalted elements proceed from this misery.

The ponderousness of which we spoke—it was our point of departure to enter more profoundly into this phenomenon—confers a special weight on all activity. Whether melancholy touches the roots of a man's being can readily be perceived. Open simplicity of life causes joy. But if a man's existence takes that other direction he can be truly conversant with people and ideas that have a tendency toward depth. Greatness, honest-to-goodness greatness, cannot be attained without that pressure which gives all things their entire weight and releases the power for effective action, without a kind of constitutional sadness called by Dante *la grande tristezza,* which arises not from any particular occasion but from existence as such.

This heaviness, this dark sadness at times bears tremendously precious fruit. When the pressure is removed and introspection opens its doors a lightness of existence arises— that soaring elevation of the entire person, that penetration of things and of life, that clarity of vision and infallibility of concept that Kierkegaard has described.

We spoke above of the urge toward concealment and quiet. This urge reveals more than the fear of meeting with a reality that can wound. In the final analysis it signifies the inner gravitation of the soul toward the great center, the impulse to seek interiority and depth, the yearning for that region where life passes from a fortuitous jumble to a protected haven where, freed from the multiplicity of individual utterances, it rests on the unicity of a solid foundation. It means a return from dissipation to a sense of the whole; from abandonment to external existence to the reserve and the custody of the sanctuary; from the superficial to the mystery of origins. The great melancholy figures yearn for the night and for a mother's arms.

Melancholy means connection with the obscure foundations of being. "Obscure" here does not mean any diminution, not the opposite of the good and beneficent light. Obscure does not signify "darkness," but the living equivalent of light. Darkness is evil, something negative. Obscurity is related to light, and both together form the mystery that is proper to man. Melancholy longs for this obscurity, convinced that the clear forms of the present will emerge from it.

In characteristic contrast to this obscurity is relationship with infinite space, with vast distances, the sea, the prairie, the lofty summits, autumn with its falling leaves and opening vistas; the mythos stretching back into infinity. Endless external space and a restricted interior communicate with one another. Both are the figure and the locale for this occurrence.

Precisely from this melancholy which devaluates things, hollows out forms and values, which makes everything unreal and thus drives itself into emptiness and loathing, which knocks away the props of existence and so rushes into the absurdity of despair—from this same despair something of Dionysian proportions bursts forth. Doubtless, the melancholy person has a most profound feeling for the fullness of

existence. The glorious colors of the world appear brighter
to him; he perceives more intimately the sweetness of the
inner sound. With his whole being he feels the power of the
world's forms. From the substance of the melancholy man
breaks forth an abundance of living energies; he is in a
position to experience the unruliness of all creation.

But always, I believe, this is bound up with goodness,
with the desire that life may manifest itself in goodness, in
friendliness, that it may prove beneficent for others.

In my opinion, the truly melancholy person cannot be
harsh by nature. He is too deeply acquainted with suffering.
True, melancholy persons have been harsh, even unmerciful.
But they always become so because of their inner misery—
their fear or despair. They are at odds with themselves.
Nothing becomes so cruel as despair which no longer knows
where to turn. Then, indeed, when the melancholy subject
loses goodness—precisely because he is so deeply implicated
in life—something particularly evil invades him, something
that is evil because of proximity, because of contact with the
nerves of life. In these circumstances he may injure others
in the same way that life inflicts pain on him. This aspect
of melancholy Kierkegaard has embodied in the figure of
Nero in *Either—Or*.

This brings us to the core of melancholy. Basically it is
a yearning for love—love in all its forms and in all its
degrees, from the most elementary sensibility to the most
exalted love of the spirit. With all its might, melancholy goes
after *eros*—the desire for love and for beauty.

This deep longing affects not only part of the being, but
proceeds from its center. It does not restrict itself to particular relationships and times, but pervades the whole. The
entire melancholy personality is permeated by *eros,* whose
special function it is to seek love and beauty together, to long
for beauty, which by itself is already very dangerous and

6

indicates a crisis in life whenever it appears. In this longing, we have the reason for the vulnerability of which we spoke. An affectionate nature is always wide open. It is ready to give and to receive. It is trusting. It does not protect itself.

Such a nature experiences the pain of transitoriness, the fact that the beloved object is taken away, that living beauty is always in a state of passing, that death is the neighbor of the beautiful.

But in stark opposition to that is the desire for the eternal, for the infinite, for the absolute. Melancholy longs for the absolutely perfect, for the unattainable, for profound and intimate values, for the untouchably exalted and noble and precious.

It desires what Plato called the proper goal of *eros*, the highest good, which at the same time is the only reality and incarnate beauty, imperishable and limitless. It seeks to perceive this reality which alone satisfies, to embrace it, to be united with it. This extraordinary phenomenon can be traced throughout the history of human groping and thought: a particularly strong feeling of the insufficiency of the finite; the will to find a way and a special intensity in the manner of gaining possession of the absolute. Mere knowledge of it does not suffice nor does assuming it ethically in actions. Here there is a yearning for union, for contact of being with being, for immersion and drinking and satisfaction, a longing for existential union.

To this end are directed those two basic drives of life which in a melancholy person have a special coloring and stand in such painful contrast to one another: the drives toward fulfillment and toward destruction—the destruction of that miserable human and earthly form of existence, so that the one may be all in all, so that therein the supreme goal of life may be achieved. On the higher level of the Christian ideal the words of St. Paul, "I live, now not I, but

Christ lives in me," express the innermost desire of that
spiritual attitude, which pays the price for it in melancholy.

It desires the absolute, but in such a way that it is the
good, the noble, that is, the special and essential characteristic of love. The melancholy person ardently wants to meet
the absolute, but as love and beauty.

IV

But again—and here we come full circle—in the melancholy
person this longing for the absolute is joined to the profound
consciousness that it cannot be attained.

The melancholy disposition has a sense and a desire for
values. It strives for the sum total of all that is precious, for
the supreme good. But it seems almost as if this yearning for
values turned against itself. For accompanying it is a feeling
of impossibility of realization. This may be the result of
specific experiences—of having failed on this occasion or
neglected duty on another, of having wasted time or missed
an opportunity that will never return. All these, however, are merely indicative of something more deep-seated,
namely, a feeling of impossibility which antecedently goes
hand-in-hand with that desire. Impossibility exists already in
the manner in which the absolute is willed—in an impatience to gain possession, in striving directly for the goal
without considering the intervening obstacles, as a result of
which an unrealistic road to the goal is pursued. That is
precisely the point: the desire for the fullness of values and
of life, for infinite beauty, is joined with a profound feeling
of transitoriness, of neglect, of loss, resulting in pain and a
restlessness that cannot be stilled—and that is melancholy.

It is like an air that surrounds everything, like a fluid
that permeates everything, like a simultaneous bitterness and
sweetness that is mixed into everything.

V

This brings us to the question of the meaning of this phenomenon and the definition of its role. Going beyond medical and pedagogical considerations, I believe it has this meaning: it is a sign that the absolute exists. The infinite makes itself felt in the heart. Melancholy is an expression of the fact that we are limited beings, that we live face to face—let us drop the too cautious and too abstract word which we have used hitherto, the "absolute," and employ the one that really belongs here—that we live face to face with God. We have been called by God, encouraged to assume him into our existence.

Melancholy may be described as the birthpangs of the eternal in man—or rather, in specified men destined to experience the pains of this birth more profoundly. Some individuals experience preeminently the natural and the human. They stand forth clearly. Their work is exactly defined; their life has its quota of joy and sorrow; their earthly situation has definite outlines. And if they do not fall victims to this danger of clarity, to comfort and to pedantry; if they understand their finiteness on a plane of infinite decisions, then their existence is beautiful and noble.

There are people who, so to say, are "on the other side" without effort, who live other-worldly lives and are strangers here, awaiting their goal. Their lives, too, are clear. The danger exists that they may become unrealistic, flippant, unstable. If they conquer this danger, if they learn faithfulness in the place assigned to them, vigilance without at the time neglecting their day's duties no matter how unimportant these may seem to them, then their existence will be clear and beautiful.

But there are also individuals who experience profoundly the mystery of limits. By nature they stand neither on this side nor on that. They live in the realm of limits. They experience the disturbance of the one sphere by the other—just as they contain the poles of what is human, its entirety, but at the same time the possibility of inner division.

Medical practitioners and psychologists offer long disquisitions on the causes and the intrinsic structure of melancholy. Naturally, their utterances are often so banal that they cannot be reconciled with the depth and the force of the experiences which accompany that phenomenon. What they say applies to the lower structural bases and goes no further. Its true meaning can be drawn only from the spiritual. And, in the final analysis, in my opinion, that meaning can be expressed as follows: melancholy is the disturbance of man caused by the proximity of the eternal. It is simultaneously blessedness and menace.

But a distinction must be made. Kierkegaard again indicates it. There is a good melancholy and an evil melancholy. Good is the one that precedes the birth of the eternal. It is the inner distress that arises from the closeness of the eternal, from the fact that it cries for realization. It is the continuous, even though unconscious, active demand to assume the infinite into one's life, to express it in disposition and action. This becomes particularly urgent when it is time, when the hour has struck, when a decision must be made or an action carried out, when a new phase must be initiated in the vital process of man, when a new breakthrough of the inner spiritual form must be realized. Such working and such becoming proceed from inner distress, which at the same time is the pressure created by the feeling of fullness; they bespeak the fear of life brought about by the claims of that which seeks to be born of it. Life feels it should submit, give up something it hitherto considered secure, submerge so that something new may go forth from it.

This working and this becoming are ascents, culminating points, where life yields its utmost. These are reached only if a man has previously passed through the depths. Creative, life-giving man differs from the conquering, possessive, domineering individual. The former brings forth, and thereby reaches heights which the latter cannot know. At the same time the question of dignity arises. He realizes that he is the instrument of powers. But he suffers a feeling of some kind of inferiority, of being somehow contemptible. Every creative man is ashamed of something. He becomes aware of it as soon as he compares himself with the non-creative man, the individual who as a result is so sure of himself, so uncomplicated. Melancholy finds this question of dignity, which goes with creativeness, a most bitter potion.

The good melancholy is made to bear and to produce. From it proceed work and activity, as a result of which everything is transformed. But if it does not find expression, if the individual cannot bring up the energy to concentrate on his work and activity, if he does not possess the generosity of sacrifice, the daring of abandonment, the power of making a breakthrough; if that which sought expression remains within or is realized very imperfectly—then the second form of melancholy, the evil one, takes over. It consists in the consciousness that the eternal did not attain the form intended for it, in the consciousness of failure, of loss. In it the danger of being damned is felt because the imposed duty was not fulfilled—that which spells eternal weal or woe but which must be executed in time, which passes and never returns. This melancholy has a different character. It is evil. It can mount to the proportions of hopelessness and despair in which man simply gives up; the idea of failure takes definitive form.

But with regard to this melancholy, too, an obligation exists. What has been done cannot be undone. What has been lost cannot be regained directly. But something more exalted remains: the appeal to the religious sphere. Purely ethical teaching says, "What has happened has happened, and you bear the responsibility. What is lost remains lost, and you bear the responsibility. See to it that you act correctly the next time." This is, however, an abstract way of putting the matter. What if we are not dealing with an abstraction but with a living subject? In the vital relationship of personal existence one day presupposes another, one action rests on the preceding one. In this case it does not do to say, "Act correctly the next time." Man cannot simply let bygones be bygones and proceed to the next action. He always acts in the totality of his being. Hence in some way or other the past must be mastered, so that the whole of life may stand at the disposition of renewal.

Now, this cannot come about by a simple ethical act, but only by the religious act which we call sorrow. By sorrow we become new beings in God's sight. True sorrow exists only in relation to the absolute, not in relation to any abstract absolute, to a bare imperative or moral law, but in relation to a living being, to God. Sorrow means that I place myself on God's side, against myself. I do not claim any self-justification, but confess my guilt—before God and with him. That is the vitalizing element. This phrase, "before God and with him," calls to life something new which cannot be analyzed. Here is a rebirth, a new coming into being. In it the faults and the mistakes of the past are not undone, but they are overcome. That which has been neglected is not mechanically rectified but is achieved anew on a higher level.

All that has been said describes the critical points in the melancholic's life. More important, because more fundamental, is gaining the higher plane on which the whole of existence can be mastered. This means coming to grips with reality. The mistake of the melancholic relationship to reality comes to the fore principally in two situations, in a twofold temptation that comes to every man but with special force to the melancholic: the temptation to yield to the call of nature and the senses and to yield to the call of the religious element.

The first temptation demonstrates a false relationship to things and to oneself. Everything, including one's own self, is considered as an intimate part of nature in which the self must live out its days; as one great whole, a single stream, a great passing from one thing to another, with no definite limits anywhere. Everything is one—one existence, one life, one birth and effort, one sensation and suffering. All multiplicity is but the expression of the one, which manifests itself in a thousand forms. From this feeling arises the tremendous temptation to plunge in, to let oneself sink according to disposition—either in sense pleasures, in experiences of all kinds, in activity or in resigned *dolce far niente,* in yielding to what appear to be invincible powers. The temptation may take the form of engaging in harried activity, in the genius of continuous production in which man feels himself an organ of nature, the place of emergence of unnameable powers, or the instrument of a vagrant spirit not confined to space. Or again, it may appear—while seemingly abandoning these connections with nature by going to the opposite extreme—as a form of titanism of spirit, of unsatisfied seeking, of an all-destroying question, of a doubt that undermines everything.

The other temptation sets up a false relationship to the absolute. That too is grasped directly, as limitlessness to be attained without further ado, as a fullness to be immediately imbibed, as a mystery into which the person continuously enters by thinking, seeing, feeling, seeking himself, as a distant goal to which a straight path leads, and, however else he may envisage the absolute with which he stands in

immediate contact, as something to be taken hold of immediately, in piety or impiety, in revolt or in submission.

In both cases the decisive element—the limit, that which
is purely human—is jettisoned. Not to be the world, but
more than the world. Not to be part of nature, but different
from it. Not to be a wave in a stream, an atom in a con-
glomerate, an organ with its connections, but spirit. To be
a person, a self-sufficient, responsible person; God's likeness,
subject to his summons, and from that standpoint free in
this world. On the other hand, the purely human does not
aspire to be God or a part of God or an organ of his pulsa-
ting spirit or anything else that would obliterate the essential
difference between God and man, but to be "absolutely less"
than he—his creature.

Man is God's creature. Hence it becomes impossible for
man without further ado to break into God, as it were; and
the attempt is forbidden. Every path to God passes through
the consciousness of the infinite difference, through reverence,
through "fear and trembling" on the part of the creature.

Man is God's likeness—in spirit and reason. As a result
it becomes impossible to be a part of nature, and the attempt
to become such is not permissible. On the contrary, man's
innermost being stands outside the world, before God,
capable and destined to hear his appeal and to answer it.

All this means that it is man's lot to be a living limit,
to recognize the fact and to live his circumscribed life. That
sets him in the realm of reality. As a result he is free of the
fascination of a false, direct oneness with God as well as a
direct identification with nature. A chasm, a two-sided cleft,
surrounds him. Thus man's way to nature is broken by a
sense of responsibility to God. Thereby his whole attitude
toward nature comes under the purview of the spirit, under
the obligation of dignity as the content of this responsibility.
His way to God is interrupted by the realization that he is

only a creature, that basically he must come to God by an act which simultaneously signifies separation and union, adoration and obedience. Every utterance about God that cannot be assimilated into adoration is false, just as all behavior toward God which cannot be assimilated into obedience is false.

Man's proper attitude is manifested precisely in this disposition—the observance of his limits, which at the same time are those of reality.

It is veracity, courage and patience. Patience above all. The solution, properly speaking, comes only from faith, from the love of God.

Only the mystery of Gethsemane—and behind it the mystery of sin with all its consequences—can supply an adequate answer: the Lord "was sorrowful unto death;" he carried his heavy burden to the end in fulfillment of his Father's will. Only in the Cross of Christ do we find the solution for the distress caused by melancholy. Time does not allow further discussion of this point; and now, at the end, the imperfections and the piecemeal character of my presentation strike me forcibly. But I shall let it stand, because I personally am not in a position to do better and because I believe that some benefit will accrue from having presented these matters as I have.

Further, it is impossible to demonstrate how profoundly questions regarding melancholy are posed, and how Christian replies to those questions are given, in the letters of St. Paul. He does so in trenchant phrases, in exclamations, in the underlying tone of his entire discussion, in the color and sound of his language. Here exists an entire theology of melancholy, pervious, of course, only to him "who has experienced."

Here, too, we can find the reply to that element of melancholy for which no solution exists on earth.

LIVING FREEDOM:
The Spirit of Man and the Spirit of God

Introduction

The essence of the present-day intellectual revival may be described in the following terms: the unity of the medieval concept of the world is dissolving. The self-evident relation in which the various fields of human existence and endeavor functioned in that unity is tending to disappear. Passing, too, is the natural way in which the thought and action of one sphere carried over into another: from the realm of faith to that of natural culture; from the ethical to the esthetic; from the philosophical to the political, and the rest. The unaffected manner in which criteria in one sphere transfer to another, the way in which the findings in one form of endeavor are accepted in another, is coming to an end. Every field strives to become autonomous. That is why each seeks to discover what differentiates it specifically from all others. It looks for a meaning proper to itself alone, for a basic value reserved to itself, for standards of authenticity applicable only to itself. It searches for norms of its own by which it can then govern its particular "critically pure" method. There is question here of the independent status of the areas of culture. This was perceived obscurely at first, but gradually it became clearer, both practically and theoretically. "Culture" is here taken in its widest meaning as the sum total of man's existence and activity when brought into living contact with his environment.

In this fashion the various fields tend to move apart, though this movement depends on their object, their sustaining activity, their determining value and specific method. Often this comes about only after a violent struggle; often there are accusations of wrongdoing, or at least of an attitude regarded as disedifying because it blasts the sanctified claims of order and tradition. All this happens with a logical consistency of purpose that becomes progressively more one-sided and embittered—a situation that our contradictory human existence seemingly cannot avoid. Thus the separate fields come to the fore. There is science, which recognizes only the methodical consequence of the search for truth as determined by the object, and art, which serves exclusively the realization of esthetical values, the perfection of expression and of form. There is politics, which regards as the sole purpose of its activity the maintenance of the State in power and well-being; economics, which recognizes no other value or criterion than the maximum of material production and consumption, and ethics, which is concerned solely "with doing good for the sake of the good," abstracting from all goals whether religious or worldly.

So vehemently does every single field press its claims that the unity of the whole is lost in the autonomy of the individual fields. A man can no longer understand what a specific political attitude has to do with individual ethics, or a specific artistic expression with the truth of knowledge. This striving for autonomy obviously has gone awry. For the sake of a legitimate partial goal—namely, to show forth the particular nature of a special field—it rejects its proper place in the sum total of objective as well as of personal relationships. The desire for "critical purity" has indeed perceived the necessity of specific self-justification, but not the equally important requirement of finding its proper slot.

Today this second aspect of the problem would seem to be to the fore: the feeling for the totality of human existence as composed of various objects, basic acts, values and criteria. It is realized that the complete independence of the various fields brought about by the desire for autonomy cannot possibly be maintained. Thus the problems of relationship, of mutual evaluation, of proper dovetailing become acute.

Living Freedom

The attempt to lay bare the philosophical foundation of Christian culture necessarily involves the problem of freedom. Inextricably united with it is the problem of necessity, employing this word in a very general sense. Both evoke a question about the roots of the human attitude embraced by those two concepts, and thus lead beyond to the problem of the spirit.

I

The process of culture comprises three elements.

First of all, there is the formable human being in his concrete actuality: existing in his own environment; having relations with other men, both individually and collectively; related to things; in vital relationship to history; a unique being existing here and now.

In addition to this there is the sum total, and the unity, of all those values and urges which seek to find expression in man, more concretely in a particular man. This we shall call the living image.

Finally, there is the formative act itself, by which that expression and formation come to fruition.

This entire process—it is a concrete unity which can be resolved into the elements just delineated by using a certain amount of violence—possesses an essential character marked by two qualities: freedom and immutability.

The formative act, whether directed toward another or concentrated on itself, proceeds from freedom and seeks to create freedom. In this way man's formation differs from the process of development to be found in a growing tree or a maturing animal. This freedom, however, derives its place, its point of departure, its goal and assurance from the immutable element.

This immutable element consists of all those components at the disposal of the developing man and of those who fashion him. These things man cannot change; indeed, if he understands and evaluates the order of things aright, he would not desire to change them. In this category belong the necessitites: ideas, values, laws, beginning with the highest and most spiritual and descending to the lowest and most material. If the formative process is to be true and genuine, then it must move in this sphere. Facts belong in the same category. A law cannot be other than what it is. A fact might indeed be different. The formula of the law of chance can never be stated in any other terms. But it need not happen that I lift this particular brick and let it fall. The action can be entirely omitted. If it does occur, unlimited possibilities offer themselves—intensity, and so on. Once it has happened, this fact then remains irrevocable. The plateau of the immutable—that plateau on which we stand, on which we grow, on which our destiny unravels itself—is woven of necessities and facts. It is also the plateau of the process of formation, and a valid pedagogy must recognize the significance of a realistic, not a visionary, effort at formation, in order to discern the immutable elements that exist and to appraise them correctly.

The ethos of the effort at formation consists in coming to terms with the immutable elements, and in arriving at an understanding of necessity and fact. In that way formation will proceed realistically. At the same time this effort requires a consciousness of freedom. To recognize freedom, to act on a basis of freedom and its responsibility, to increase and expand freedom—all this belongs just as much to man's deepest instincts as does respect for the immutable elements. A consideration of this connection will lead to a discussion of the nature of freedom.

Here I should like to add something by way of preamble.

Any discussion of the question of freedom is burdened with age-old controversies. These cannot be weighed properly unless the interior attitude has first been purified. We shall attempt it by the following brief reflection:

All knowledge requires presuppositions if it is to succeed. The cognitive power is not a mechanical apparatus, but a living potentiality. The cognitive process cannot be likened to the focussing of photographic apparatus, which mechanically reproduces what exists before the lens. Thought in the abstract does proceed thus. And this holds true of thought in general, of the subject in general, directed to an object in general. It is an empty schema, but reality is quite different. In reality, there is the concrete thought of this living person directed toward this determined thing. Now, this is a concrete, living act. It may or it may not succeed. Its success depends on very definite presuppositions: whether the concrete subject who is living in this act of thinking stands where he must stand in order to grasp this object; whether he has the kind of interior disposition demanded, that special adaptability of his plastic organic power to the object required by this class of objects, this realm of reality. All this differs with different objects that are to be comprehended.

It is again quite different if there is question of a logical, mathematical relationship or of an essential image. The former, for example, a mathematical or a physical law, can be deduced. The latter—for example, that iron "exists" and that iron shows forth a congeries of qualities: its particular color, hardness, weight and so on—cannot be deduced, but in the last analysis only noted, understood and accepted. If the hearer only had the readiness and determination never to accept anything, this ultimately would mean that A $\neq$ A; if, on the other hand, he had the readiness and determination not to close his mind to anything, which in the last analysis means that A $=$ A, then he can be induced to accept purely logical relationships.

In the case of the essential image, the matter is different. In order to grasp that any one particular thing is as it is, in order to comprehend the significance of its particular mode of existence, more is required than the readiness to think logically. A qualitative determination, an essential image, forces itself upon consciousness not by a formal, logical necessity but by the impetus of its being contrary to our being, by the power which the determinateness of its mode of being exercises on our susceptibility. However, in order that this impetus, this power should come to fruition, a readiness must pre-exist: namely, a readiness to perceive whatever is proper and particular in things, a readiness to accept everything, and more particularly the thing in question, as it is. We must not prescribe how it ought to be but let it express itself freely by its own being. This appears self-evident, but it is not. Far from it! In reality we do not open ourselves to the world as it exists, but we demand that it conform to our desires. Our self-assertiveness desires things to be such that we feel ourselves assured, protected, sustained and advanced by them. In this way we continually strive to make the world conformable to our particular being.

Every glance at the world as it exists in itself causes a tension in my being. Every thing has essential aspects that are foreign to my particular endowment. There are entire fields of being that are strange to my self-will. Indeed, in myself I discover aspects that disagree with the dominant element of my being. To consider things as they are always leads to my feeling more uncomfortable in the world. As a result, I find it more rewarding to exist in this world of which—if I understand myself rightly—I must constantly say, "Thank God, it is not as I would wish it to be!"

All this holds true of freedom in a special measure. It makes some difference to me whether there is freedom. A very important part of my being would rather see that none existed. I can live more comfortably if there is no freedom. All that the word "responsibility" connotes vanishes as soon as there is none. In a pre-eminent way the question of freedom demands preparation for the encounter with reality, the readiness to comprehend it and to accept it.

II

And now we put the question: Does freedom exist?

We want to be certain that we understand the question correctly. Only too often it is sketched out in a preliminary way, in an abstract manner, in such a way as to become fruitless. It is phrased as follows: Can an action come about without causal necessity? And from this follows the usual sterile disputation. In truth, we are dealing not with an abstract problem but with a concrete reality. And therefore we must have recourse to that which alone can furnish information concerning reality, namely, experience.

We can put the matter this way: Does my inner experience supply me with a procedure, a form of action, a relationship to the object and to myself which has a special character, different from all other procedures, forms of action and manners of relationship—a character I can only describe by the word "freedom"?

This, then, is the picture. Freedom exists. More precisely, I, a concrete person, feel myself free. Just as my inner experience apprises me of the fact that I am conscious, capable of knowing myself and really knowing about myself, so likewise my inner experience shows me that I am free. This freedom is a fact, a concrete fact, a real condition, a living attitude, a manner of my human being's existing and acting. And, abstracting from the former, I experience the fact that free action and existence abide in me.

With a part of my being and activity I am embedded in the pervading causality of nature; I am a piece, a member. At the same time I am aware of something in me, something living and real, not only ideal and intelligible, that is self-sustaining. To put it more exactly, therein I stand.

With a part of my being and activity I am the effect of cause, the result of premises. To that extent I belong not to myself but to general forces. But something in me belongs to itself. More precisely, therein I belong to myself.

With a part of my being I am the channel for various events: the transformation of impulses that come from the outside and again proceed to the outside. But I also experience that I am the origin of events. More precisely, I experience myself as the living origin of activities, as the source of causal relationships.

The fact that I experience myself, regarded in this special sense, as existing in myself, as belonging to myself, as the origin of activities, I express by the phrase, "I know I am free." I am not free completely, not always, and not always to the same degree. But I am in this sense free with respect to what is most profound, most proper to my being; I am in this sense free at times; I am free in varying degrees.

The fact of this freedom, the living possibility of realizing it, the possibility and the duty of developing it, of purifying its activity and enlarging its scope—all of this forms a basic characteristic of my human and personal existence.

In free action, however, freedom can be experienced variously.

There is the experience of free choice: I become conscious of the possibilities of different courses of action; I consider them; I weigh them; I decide on one of them. The character of freedom lies in my ability to choose from among the various possibilities those that I want. No doubt, there are reasons, motives: I go this way because it is shorter ; I go the shorter way because I wish to attain my goal quickly; I want to reach the goal because I have something important to perform there, and so on. Freedom does not consist in having at hand motives and reasons more or less clearly indicated, but in the manner in which these reasons or motives come to be realized. When I have given the chain of reasons in a physical or biological procedure, then I am finished, and the whole thing closes with a "because" whose content is determined by the specific causes or congeries of causes.

In free action, however, a further question is possible: why do I allow this reason, this motive, to be determinative? The answer runs: because I so choose. The line of reasoning enters into the question of the choosing ego's sovereignty. This is not caprice, not irrationality, but it truly is the reason. And indeed an entirely adequate reason. Here the action stands by itself. Or rather, the agent stands by himself. He made the beginning, and this beginning is then drawn immediately into the web of the naturally effective causes.

By the fact that I experience myself as a sovereign chooser, as the master of my decisions, I experience my freedom. I am free to the degree that I exercise mastery over my decisions, that I rise above the matter at hand. The ultimate term of this freedom—really an impossibility— would be a decision based on complete lack of consideration of the vital possibilities. (Compare the ethos of the Stoics and the psychological basis of the ascetical "holy indifference.")

I discover still another facet of the experience of freedom in myself: I am not disinterested in it. This essential freedom does not sit in judgment, deciding on either hand. With it I have the consciousness that qualitatively the action proceeds from my innermost being. Freedom of choice had a formal character. I experienced freedom in proportion to my interior disinterestedness, in proportion to my independence of the object and the effective motives. It was a dispositive freedom, freedom of choice. Here the situation is different. The acting ego stands in an elementary relationship to the content of the activity. I find myself free in it to the degree that the action proceeds more completely, more intimately, from what I am. I experience the greatest freedom in an action where "I cannot act otherwise." Naturally, this has nothing to do with physical or psychical compulsion; not being able to act otherwise does not signify being forced. It means, rather, that the entire living person enters into the activity, that I express myself immediately in it—and I do so with what is most intimate, most proper to me, with the very core of my being. In other words, I then act in accord with my being.

Here, then, I experience myself as free if the action proceeds from my innermost being with qualitative immediacy, if I enter wholly into this action with what is most proper to me.

Of course, man's inner self is not univocal. There is a "true" inner self and a "false" inner self, just as by free choice I can do right or wrong. Thus essential freedom, just as the freedom of choice, receives its definite determination only by what it comprises. (More about that later.)

If we would want to express the experience of freedom

very tersely we might say, freedom means belonging to one-self. I experience myself as free when I realize that I belong to myself, that in my action I am master of myself, that the action does not merely pass through me and therefore belong to another jurisdiction, but that it originates in me, that consequently it is mine in a special sense, and that I am my own in it.

The manner in which I experience this self-possession bifurcates into the two types I have just mentioned. I learn that I belong to myself in the sovereignty of independent choice; and I learn that I belong to myself in that process which expresses my innermost being in action. In the first case I learn that I am master of myself; in the second, that I am my own self.

Which side the experience of freedom will lean toward in an individual case depends on psychological structure. There are arguments for the view that in freedom of choice the masculine form of the experience of freedom comes to the fore; the feminine in the expression of being. But at least to a slight degree both will always be present simultaneously. And this fact, that both always play a role, points up the concrete, antithetical structure of the experience of freedom.

What we have said hitherto refers to freedom as a concrete act, more precisely, as the form of concrete acts. This is psychological freedom.

Special importance attaches to it, because here the decision is made whether the phenomenon of freedom will be accepted clearly and with all its consequences, or whether the matter will take flight into an undetermined and transcendental sphere. Psychological freedom consists in my possessing the sovereignty of choice as an actual, living concrete being. It lies in my ability to decide on the basis of a point of departure which itself is no longer a point of transition in a causal series. It signifies that I possess a capability not merely for natural, but for spiritual and creative self-expression. Psychological freedom implies that in my activity I belong to myself—not always, not always in the same measure, but in specific cases and to a certain degree.

I possess this psychological freedom both as endowment and as possibility. But as a living reality it must be achieved. Freedom of choice is not assured without further ado. If there is to be genuine choice and not merely capitulation to any sort of motive, then interior uprightness and consistent practice are demanded. A man must free himself for freedom. Similarly, freedom as an expression of being does not come about automatically. If it really is to express being and be more than a manifestation of some sort of peripheral situation, then it presupposes interior veracity and the power of self-conquest.

Freedom itself is something that exists simultaneously in the dialectic of the things that exist and those that have been sacrificed. It is a point of departure, for if I am not essentially free I can never become free. Only on the basis of freedom can a man work toward freedom; with it something new begins. It becomes actual only through activity, through practice, through formation. Freedom itself is a habit that must be achieved, that must be developed.

III

Psychological freedom is the living perfection of acts, the special character which particular acts and the attitude proceeding from them bear. But psychological freedom does not exhaust the fact of freedom. Indeed, it is only the lesser part of freedom as such. The mere possibility of free choice is something abstract. It receives living meaning only when

I ask: Free choice about what, for what purpose? Likewise, the simple possibility of expressing being is something abstract. It receives meaning only when I ask: What shall I express freely? Thus the consideration of the content of freedom—axiological freedom—is added to that of psychological freedom or the freedom of action. Only when these two are joined together—namely, freedom as the perfect form of the act and the content of the act so performed—does "living" freedom become a fact.

This is merely a particularized example of the general fact of life. Living signifies not only event and act, but also content of event and of act. When I say, "I am alive," this could mean in the first place: I exist, I can move, I feel, I have initiative, I am awake, I enjoy, I suffer, I work, and so on. The statement "I feel" acquires full significance only when I say, "I feel this." The statement "I work" becomes complete when I say, "I am working at this." The statement "I am alive" communicates its full sense when I say, "I am living this content." Thereby a basic tension of our existence finds expression: namely, that life does not merely go ahead, but becomes meaningful through its content. Our existence and activity and suffering and possessing and working acquire their proper meaning only by reason of the content they realize. It is in this way that the fact of being alive and life itself are related to an object, to the world of objects, to the world of reality and value. The objective, the real, the necessary comes into life as an essential element of it. In this connection freedom of action signifies that the relationship to the object can be correct or false, right or wrong, positive or negative. But a relationship always comes about. And therein lies the root of something tragic in the basic endowment of human living.

The same holds true here. Freedom as a whole signifies a realized object—a right and proper object—in the expression of psychological freedom. In other words, freedom means the realization of the requisite world-order in the expression of psychological freedom.

This freedom of content now extends over into various fields. We shall describe them briefly; in the course of our exposition the nature of freedom of content will become clearer.

In the first place, there is the field of freedom of things. It is the freedom of the object understood according to its essence. This consists in seeing and grasping things correctly and according to their nature.

For example, if I have to handle a tool with which I am not acquainted at all or only partially, this hinders me. In other words, I am not free, I am impeded; this tool is somewhat at odds with me. As soon as I have understood it and use it aright, a certain tension disappears. I am now free in the use of this tool. All things, all relations to objects, all natural processes have specific qualities; they show forth a plan, a form of activity. They are ordered. If I do not know that order, if I do not satisfy it by my attitude, then by that very fact and in that precise measure it becomes an obstacle to me. Friedrich Vischer in his book, *Auch Einer*, describes a man who never attains to an understanding of things. They are at odds with him. In fact, he feels they are inimical to him. He experiences "the treachery of the object." He lives in a world in which everything acts as a hindrance. Space is filled with obstacles—things that are never correctly understood.

As soon as I grasp the thing correctly, however, my working impulse can flow into it. The thing lends itself to the goal of my activity, and I cooperate with its purpose. It becomes an open channel for my activity; in other words, I discover that I am free in this thing—free for the particular possibilities at hand. It makes no difference whether this thing is a tool (the feeling of expansion and freedom coming from an instrument rightly used), or a means of conveyance (freedom of governed movement), or the vegetative laws of plants or the instincts of animals (the particular freedom with which the expert moves among them and makes them serviceable to himself), or anything else. It is the freedom of the function in accord with nature, of the correct position, of the suitable structure—taking these terms in their ordinary sense, in their meaning for life. By the very fact that man gains this freedom with regard to the right use of things, the world becomes a cosmos for him. If he does not achieve it, the world remains chaos for him; it is composed of nothing but obstacles and crisscrossing events. If he does gain this freedom the earth presents a liberating order to him; it becomes enlarged because everywhere function finds its place.

In the realm of this freedom of things belongs our own bodily and spiritual existence—the fact that we are, that we move, that we behave as the inner laws of our body and spirit dictate. Here we find the proper meaning of rhythmic formation. The body is heavy, dull, stands in its own way; man trips over his own feet as long as he has not awakened, freed and brought into play the laws of his organic existence, as long as he has not come to the point of understanding things correctly and using them correctly. Here again lies the value of the vocational school.

A higher realm is that of freedom of values. Here, just as on the aforementioned plane, we have to deal with content. Freedom does not mean release from something, but rather release for something, fulfillment in something. The psychological possibility of choice finds its fulfillment in the correct choice, in the fact that by the correct decision the living person enters into the liberating content. Thus, freedom of value consists in freedom in a value correctly appraised.

As soon as I acquire knowledge, I gain truth—this determined truth. Such truth immediately possesses meaning in itself, namely, that I have grasped the particular object correctly. At the same time, however, all acquisition of truth brings a kind of bonus with it. More precisely, it offers a sign that truth has been found. Every acquisition of truth, abstracting entirely from the matter with which it deals, works as a liberation. In the recognition of truth something in me becomes master of itself, something in me becomes conscious, is loosed, expands, develops, achieves the proper sphere in which it can live. That in me which desires truth, my spirit hungering for knowledge, feels itself confined as long as it has not acquired knowledge. It experiences expansion, not liberation, as soon as it gains truth. The tremendous experience of the expansive power lies at the basis of the attitude, say, of Socrates.

Something similar occurs through contact with the perfected form of a work of art. The meaning of the work of art consists in the fact that its essence, something hidden, is expressed in form. But not in the sense that one must stand before it. The ultimate attitude with regard to a work of art does not consist in gazing at it from a distance. A work of art rather demands that a person enter into it. A person must be intimate with it; the formed and forming entity takes hold of him and fashions him. This entrance into the moulded and spiritual realm of art likewise produces the experience of expansion.

A corresponding assertion can be made about law, about order, and so on. The realization and attainment of spiritual values exert a liberating action. Abstracting from the consideration that every independent value as such satisfies me, fulfills me with a particular sense of value, the conquest itself of the value comes as an expansive experience. This will grow in proportion to the passion with which I long for it. The world of spiritual values is a world of freedom.

If I experience the freedom of things, their constitution and their activity, by the living structure of my body and soul, then it is the living organ of world-comprehension—of the desire for values, of the consciousness of values, or whatever name you wish to give it—by which I experience the freedom of values. It connotes a living love of values, joined with a judgment of values and consciousness of values. In the last analysis, it is Platonic *eros,* which then also experiences Platonic freedom.

The world of this freedom is order, the cosmos of values. Perhaps it would be better to say that it is reality sated and filled with values.

A third realm is that of personal freedom. This can be achieved only in the two basic attitudes of solitude and of community.

As soon as I enter into the relationship with another person which has been allotted to him and to me, I experience it as something comforting, fulfilling and assuring. This sort of thing may assume the most varied forms: friendship, association in work, service, discipleship, love. There may be special forms of attachment, fulfilling particular relationships of life. These relationships I experience as particularly liberating. The fact that I occupy a position with regard to another person that is here and now right and equitable, means that I gain expansiveness, an area of movement, freedom. Every correct utterance of "you" and "we" that proceeds from the exigency of the personal situation creates freedom. Therein I am "we"; in the complete personal complex I am what I essentially must be if I am to realize my own ego. Even a clear and accurate antagonism produces this "communal freedom." To speak in Nietzschean terms, there is a "good enemy," a "good antagonist," who makes decent antagonism and clear struggle possible. On the contrary, every disordered, crooked relationship, every unfulfilled, inhibited, unredeemed relationship, binds a man; it creates obstacles and cramps the individual. Here the experience of freedom is purer and stronger in proportion as there is present less organizational order or only a generic, natural order. It increases when the relationship in question proceeds from a personal decision; it becomes more profound when the personal equation enters into the relationship. Certain areas of being actuate themselves in me, are as it were born, only when I meet the person in question occasionally, and thus bring the correct relationship with him into realization. The most intensive form of the experience of freedom comes from love.

By contrast, there is the realization of freedom in solitude. It is here that "I become conscious of myself." True, I am always myself; somehow I am always in possession of myself. Then again I am on the way to realizing myself. All genuine aloneness is a step toward my true self, a deeper grasp of my ego. I acquire perception of myself. I become a living center. The point of departure and the goal of the vital process reveal themselves. There is an enlargement in depth and breadth. The inner "spot whereon I stand" comes to the fore. To the degree that this occurs, something releases itself; the personal center quietly becomes present, becomes free.

In the two poles of aloneness and of community—considering both not abstractly but on the basis of the concrete reality of what I am and what my neighbor is, from the totality of the relationship, taking time and environment into consideration—personal freedom realizes itself. This is the freedom of "you" and "we" and of the whole, freedom of the ego.

Here, too, an order of freedom is realized. We spoke before about the cosmos of objective things and of the unity of man in it—man freed, composed of body and soul; then about the cosmos of values and of realities filled with values, a cosmos in which love of values and consciousness of values play a great part. Now we stand face to face with the well-ordered cosmos of man, in which the solitude of aloneness and the community of companionship are realized in accord with their true nature and in which the living person moves at ease, having attained his freedom.

The fourth realm of freedom, by reason of content, is the moral. This is experienced in the fulfillment of moral duties.

The morally obligatory is the good. This does not fall into the same category as truth, justice and beauty, but is realized in other values. The good is the correct and right thing in any given situation. To the question "What is the good?" Thomas Aquinas answers as follows: that which is reasonable here and now, that is, that which is called for in the concrete situation. It will be truth when there is question of knowledge; it will be beauty when there is question of the artist's creation; it may be the correct relationship to a person, to a work, to an obligation or anything else.

As soon as I do what is right and thus fulfill a duty, I experience liberation. A lie may help me to escape from a particular difficulty and so free me in a superficial stratum of existence, but a deeper stratum of my being is bound by it. I feel pressed down, burdened. The bad conscience, which accuses me of not having done what I ought, has the character of an experience of enslavement, of bondage. Immoral conduct leads to servitude—an immediate consciousness of the moral sphere which finds its definitive meaning and seal in the religious concept of slavery to Satan.

On the contrary, when I speak the truth I experience liberation. Something in me rises, expands. By every moral activity, my moral ego enlarges. Something very intimate becomes master of itself. It has the right relation to things as they ought to be, to the moral order.

A new cosmos comes into being—a cosmos in which things and persons possess not only a correct, functional, economic, cultural or personal value, but a moral one, the ethical world.

The experience of moral freedom grows in proportion to the interior or exterior obstacles which correct activity must conquer, in proportion to the purity of the person's moral code, his determination to do right, in proportion to the clarity and depth of the moral impregnation of the living person. Moral freedom finds its perfection when man does good not only from one act to another but so that it becomes part and parcel of him, when he achieves virtue in the strict sense of the word, when he not only acts morally, but is moral. That man has become definitely free whose living existence coincides with moral obligation in such a way that he can no longer do evil. But this is a perfection that cannot be achieved on earth. (Union with God in everlasting life includes *non posse peccare*.)

The final field of freedom is the religious sphere.

Man's being is most profoundly marked by the fact that although he is relative, finite, transient, he strives for the absolute, the infinite, the eternal. He does not find the ultimate, the infinite and the eternal in himself. He discovers it in his meeting with God. The rightly exercised religious act signifies a relationship to God, a relationship in which God becomes the living content of this human life. Religious acts may assume any form: adoration, thanksgiving, petition, sorrow, fear, desire, but in every instance they bring it about that somehow man comes to God, becomes a partaker of God. And if this is not actually so, still it is in accord with the inner meaning and direction of those acts. But it is precisely in this that man's religious core—that which we signify not by the psychological but by the religious term "soul"—experiences most intimately liberation as a result of this meeting. The approach to God satisfies that inner longing, both from the standpoint of psychology and of content, whatever form this partaking of God may take. Man attains to an infinite, eternal, definitive content of life without ceasing to be what he is, namely, man. This partaking of the infinite can no longer be lost, but it remains a mystery. The concept of the soul's image of God and its ability to comprehend God (the *capacitas Dei* of St. Augustine) are only descriptions of it, not solutions. This partaking breaks the last bond—the bond that lies in creaturehood itself, in simple finiteness, but without destroying creaturehood or merely throwing a deceptive veil over it. Partaking of God's infinity, of his eternal, definitive, holy life constitutes the ultimate expansion, fulfillment, satisfaction.

This must not be taken in a quantitative sense, as if infinite greatness, because it exceeds the finite absolute, signified freedom for the latter. God as God, his essence, that which he is, that which according to St. Thomas can never be completely known or thoroughly comprehended but which comes to the fore in every religious experience—this gives proper meaning to the elements of eternity, of infinity, of finality. God is he who gives to the man who approaches him definitive fulfillment and by the same token definitive liberation.

All of this finds its perfection in revelation, in Christianity. One of the subjects on which the New Testament speaks the final word is the freedom of the children of God. This can be understood only in connection with rebirth and love. In baptism and in genuine sorrow the Father admits the man of good will to a share in the divine life, to filiation. And as the most profound vital power of this new existence he confers on him that power which constitutes the mystery of his own life—the power to love. Not what is called love in the purely psychological or ethical sense, but what Jesus expressed by the word "love." This love is the disposition of God and, as a gift of grace, that of God's child. It confers ultimate freedom. For everything created constitutes by that very fact a burden, a statute, a commandment. Our entire life is subject to laws, beginning with those of nature and reaching to the sublimest laws of the spirit. Naturally, on every new plane of being the concept of "law" receives a new quality. I encounter these laws and they bind me, and ultimately every bond spells a lack of freedom. But all these laws, just as the creature in which and for which they exist, represent the work and the will of God.

As a creature, man is subject to this law. He is a "slave," as Paul says. But the moment that I become a child of God, and become such also by my disposition, at the moment when I love—when I love God, and in him both men and things— at that very moment I step to God's side and live by him. Then I desire in him all that is, and the law which was made for it. But now the law no longer is "law," but becomes the content and form of my own willing. Now, to speak again with Paul, I am "lord." That is the "freedom of the children of God"—a freedom attained not by the abolition of law, but by its ultimate fulfillment. To put it more exactly: it is a freedom gained by the fact that God allows me to approach him, the lawgiver. As a result, I am no longer "faced" by the law, but I bear it in my own will as God's gift. By this participation, granted by grace, in the love of the legislative will of the Father, his child goes over to the side of the legislator; he becomes—by grace, not by essence, be it noted—a kind of co-legislator.

This freedom, too, constructs a world. But here the word "world" disappears, to be replaced by a personal expression. The order in which love and the freedom obtained by love has the mastery, in which man assumes an attitude proceeding from God's view of men and things, is "the kingdom of God." It is the order in which the will of God is carried out "on earth." But, be it well noted, also as it is done "in heaven," that is, as it is fulfilled by those who stand on God's side. For them God's will no longer is something foreign, but the very heart of their own will. That is why this is the principal petition in the Lord's Prayer.

It need hardly be added that this also constitutes the goal of the striving of our earthly existence, particularly at the moment of eternal union with God. Christian life, after all, is travelling toward God.

IV

The entire phenomenon of freedom forms a synthesis. Freedom is that form in which man in his actions belongs to himself. Expression of that self-possession is the consciousness of having to enter upon it in a special way: imputation, both in a positive and in a negative sense; value and guilt; responsibility. This self-possession has a twofold aspect: autonomy of choice and of expression of one's being. But this autonomy remains formal, a mere incident, an act, unless we put these questions to ourselves: What is the content of our autonomy? What are we to choose freely? What kind of being are we to express? What content should our free actions have? What object should they deal with? What effect should they produce?

Freedom of content really gives meaning to psychological freedom: the freedom of execution. This freedom of execution is the realization of the freedom of content.

Culture signifies the formation of man; it proceeds from freedom and leads to freedom. It is not formation to what he must be, as with the animal and the plant—that would be merely fulfillment of the law of nature—but a formation to what he ought to be, that is, what is imposed on him as the content of freedom. For that reason this content cannot be realized in a manner imposed by nature, as in the case of the animal and the plant. It must be striven for in continually repeated free actions of choice and of expression of being, in continually repeated conquests of self. In this manner freedom becomes the presupposition, the atmosphere and the goal of the pedagogical world.

Naturally, we do not want to forget that pedagogical activity is founded just as deeply in the immutable, in fact and in law.

And so there quite logically arises a question about the relationship of freedom and immutability. This poses one of the most profound questions about the interpretation of the world; an attempt will be made later to elucidate it.

Freedom and Immutability

I

The preceding investigation concerned itself with "living freedom," and tried to view it in its whole perspective as a "living" phenomenon, as act and content, as psychological and contentful freedom.

Such freedom exists. Our human existence rests on it.

Education and culture also have their basis in it. Living culture proceeds from freedom and leads to freedom.

In the same connection mention was made of immutability. Just as there is freedom so there is immutability.

Let us speak of the immutability of the fact.

First of all, I am living today and not at an earlier or later period; I was born in this country and not in another; I have specific characteristics, such as size and limits of ability. Concrete environment to a great extent is fact; so, too, are historical locus, birth, lot in life. All these things could be different. They need not be as they are. There is no reason to assert that they have to be so, that they could not be otherwise.

We are aware of that. We sense it whenever reality goes contrary to our wishes or does not completely satisfy us. This holds particularly true when something valuable has been shattered, when something has been irretrievably lost, when a reasonably desired thing has become impossible of attainment because of external obstacles or limitations.

In a particular manner we become conscious of the importance of the factual when it proceeds from our own activity. If I have done something I should not have done, the result is a fact. It did not have to be. I know I could have omitted the action. But now it exists. It can no longer be obliterated. It is an indelible fact which produces its effects for me and for others—and produces them inevitably.

We cannot comprehend why fact has to exist and to exist in this way. Still it is there ineffaceably, inescapably actual, definitely effective. Care must be had, however, lest a person be deceived by a superficial view of casuality drawn from natural science. Certainly, many causes—sociological, historical, biological, physiological, and so on—account for my being what I am and for the constituent elements and presuppositions of my life. But all this—abstracting entirely from the diverse character of these "laws"—only implies that if this happens, that follows, that when this occurs, it comes about in a particular manner. This postulates necessity, namely, that of the "laws" in question. But that "this" should happen calls for no necessity. We are faced with something absolutely impenetrable, namely, that the world exists at all, that it is thus and not otherwise, that it has these properties and dimensions, and not others. A man has to dull his elementary metaphysical feelings as empiricism does with its adoration of physical laws, or delude them as pantheism does, in order not to see the point: in the final analysis our existence is a fact, not necessity. Therein lies the root of the tragedy. It is solved solely by faith not only in God the creator, but also in this God who is love and a father.

In this sense our entire existence rests on facts. Constantly new facts evolve about us, all of them of significance for us. Constantly we, too, produce new facts, and thus we create immutabilities in our own life and in the lives of others. Such facts constitute immutability.

There is still another species of the immutable, namely, necessity.

By necessity we understand that which must be so, which cannot be otherwise, where it is patent that it has to be thus. It is that which rests on a "law." In this category belong mathematical, chemico-physical, biological, psychological, historical, cultural, logical and metaphysical laws among others.

This form of immutability likewise determines our existence. Our life revolves around these laws.

We must clearly contemplate the importance of the immutable element—fact and necessity, fact and law—from the viewpoint of culture related to reality. The ethos of freedom belongs to the essence of culture; but so does the ethos of immutability. There is a pedagogical attitude toward freedom that has no relation to the immutable, namely, pedagogical idealism in the questionable sense of the word. It is an attitude governed solely by the feeling of freedom, by the feeling that everything is possible, that everything can be overcome, done, changed, manipulated. This feeling, however, exists without any external relationship to actual reality. We are speaking here of imaginary and not of genuine freedom. Here the educative act proceeds in a remarkably unrealistic and consequently ineffective manner. Postulates are set up, but they are purely idealistic; contrived methods are proposed. Man as he is does not enter into the picture. The pedagogical act is carried out with regard to a purely imaginary person. As a result, it does not "take"; it glances off. It is doomed to failure. Everything remains imaginary, fanciful, exaggerated, and consequently collapses. If the power of freedom is to be real it must receive a foundation from consciousness of the immutable, from a true comprehension of existing things—of that which cannot be otherwise, of real powers, of real limits, of the way in which events come about, of the manner in which things are realized. Napoleon Vallentin defines the expert in historical and political affairs as one who knows how to act so that every act of war, let us say, becomes transformed into a lasting political reality. This holds true also of every kind of work of man, particularly of artistic endeavor. The sensation of freedom solidifies freedom, and from there proceeds the genuinely creative attitude of education—pedagogical realism.

Immediately a question arises. Can these two, freedom and immutability, coexist? Does not the one cancel out the other? Are we not fictitiously combining things that are in truth mutually exclusive?

Here lies the problem of freedom.

II

Let us formulate the problem. Does the free act itself fall under necessity? Has the free act itself a law?

Naturally, as a concrete, real act it works according to the law of natural sequence. If I voluntarily lift a stone and permit it to fall, the lifting and dropping occur according to biological and psychological laws of function and the law of gravity. The free, accomplished deed from the first moment of its concrete fulfillment enters into the sphere of laws as they apply to all acts.

If we stop there, however, the problem has not yet been fully grasped. We have to go back to the origin and ask whether the first beginning, the inception of the freely performed act, by reason of its active principle, also has a law. Here lies the real problem.

In order not to be confused by a multiplicity of forms, let us reduce to one simple basic form everything that goes by the name of "law," that is, everything that signifies necessity of occurrence. More exactly, we want to try the problem by the simplest form of legality which is contained in every higher form—the law of sufficient reason.

This law means that everything that exists and that happens has a sufficient reason for existing and happening, and for existing and happening in just this way.

This law finds application always and everywhere. It is an axiom of our thought process and a basic form of our existence. Taken universally, as we have done, the law remains uniform everywhere, irrespective of the object to which it is applied in an individual case.

But there is another question. Does this same situation, namely, that everything that happens has a sufficient reason for happening, retain its identical character in the various spheres of human existence? It is evident that sufficient reason exists everywhere. Is the manner in which this sufficient reason acts evident in the same way? What if we no longer consider this most common form of the law, but its concrete reality? The law as such does not exist; it is an abstraction. What does exist is the concrete thing and the concrete happening. But is the manner in which a happening affects this thing "with sufficient reason," hence the concrete execution of the sufficient reason, everywhere the same if we contemplate it in the various aspects of reality?

For here is a fact which, in our opinion, becomes progressively more obvious in the egalitarian attempts of our mechanistic age: things are not uniform. The generalized abstraction assists thought. But reality presents immense variety. Individual things are distinguished from one another; particularly distinct are the realms of the real.

Let us trace the course by which a happening progresses from its active causes through the various gradations of reality.

There is a mode of thought which has for its express or implied axiom: all existing things form a unity. Basically it denies qualities, since these do not permit themselves to be cumulated. So it becomes mechanistic and quantitative. Is that "axiom" really true? It will be difficult to determine anything definite here. Let us omit discussion of the matter, and instead ask by way of approach if greater possibility of comprehension, both with regard to breadth of field as well as to the characteristics, purity and fullness of phenomena, is offered when we proceed from the supposition that existence is uniform, or from the supposition that it is varied? that it is only one or that it has a multiplicity of data which ultimately cannot be referred to one another? The former supplies the basis for unitarian, the latter for pluralistic thinking. They mutually accuse one another of grave faults. The former says that the pluralistic way of thinking produces chaos; the latter asserts that the unitarian manner impoverishes. In fact, we meet here antithetical types of existence and of thought, and an important structural problem of thought itself.

I believe that for us here and now the pluralistic mode is more pressing. We need to free our gaze. And we have the duty to regard this pluralism not as something anarchic, but as being "in order," which in this context signifies not only hierarchic order. Monarchical and democratic order exist even in the lowest ranks.

There is the field of inanimate nature, as considered by physics, chemistry, astronomy, and so on. What do we mean in this field when we say that a process has a sufficient reason? In order to pinpoint the problem, let us direct it to this question: When do I come to a comprehension of the sufficient reason for a particular process?

As soon as we seek the answer, we notice that we must make distinctions. The objective situation contains two considerations: the quantitative and the qualitative. And each of them has to be regarded differently.

The quantitative signifies that a thing, a process, has this mass, this extension, this intensity of energy; that these changes take place in these particular degrees. In this area the question of sufficient reason is, Why do we find this size, this mass? The question is answered if I can demonstrate that the magnitude of the effect can be traced to the magnitude of the cause. This comes about necessarily and cannot be otherwise. As a result, I can deduce one magnitude from the other. The means of this deduction is mathematics; its product, the mathematical theory of the sciences.

Here, however, a difficulty arises. True, mathematics is simply and commonly regarded as the expression of scientific exactitude because it has to do with masses and their relationship, hence with quantities. Does this square with the facts?

Apparently not. Is the circle only something quantitative, the expression of the fact that an infinite number of points are equidistant from a common point of reference? Is the circle not rather a form? But a form is not something quantitative. More exactly, it has a quantitative law, that of the mass-relationship of the circle. But in itself it is something qualitative; here we consider the circle as a specified datum of sight. It cannot, however, be deduced, for example, by comparison of size with distance. As soon as the distances of the peripheral points from the center are compared as far as form is concerned, this in reality is already presupposed as bearing a qualitative phenomenon.

Indeed, even the algebraic formula appears to be more than an expression of quantities. It, too, is a "form," albeit not a visible one. Rather, it represents a total picture of relationships, and this signifies not just a simple comprehension of sizes, but a bearer of character, a bearer with a significance of essence.

But where do we find the sufficient reason for the origin of the mathematical relationships that bear character? Not in the quantities of the cause. They can lie only in the qualitative element. Quality, however, cannot be derived from quality; it "appears."

Let us return to the point of departure. We saw that the quantitative element of a process is understood in its sufficient reason if the size of the cause can be deduced. The inanimate object, however, consists not only of quantities; it also has properties.

If, by means of pressure and temperature changes, a gas first turns into a liquid and then into a solid, where do we find the sufficient reason for the successive properties? Not for the mass that comes into being, namely, the volume, but for the qualities of the various aggregate conditions—gaseous, liquid, solid—abstracting entirely from color, taste, and so on? The natural scientist leans to the opinion that these alleged qualities are something quantitative, presumably the varying speed in the movement of the atoms, their varying density in space, and so on. With all due respect, that is an error in observation! Fluidity is not synonymous with determined degrees of movement and density; fluidity is simply fluidity. And even though I know that the figures for the mass of movement and density in the fluid state can be deduced from the corresponding figures in the gaseous state, as soon as specified figures of pressure and temperature are added, I still know nothing at all about the qualities of the fluid condition! I possess the sufficient reason for its quantities, not for its qualities. Precisely here we find the difference between Goethe's and Newton's view of nature! I may know the formulae for all chemical and physical transformations, but as a result I still do not have a single quality or a single change of quality!

A quality simply cannot be deduced. It cannot be deduced from a quantity because these two concepts differ essentially. A thing cannot be deduced from something unrelated. Hence quality can only be established qualitatively. The reason for the qualities of the effect resides in the qualities of the cause. Must, therefore, the qualities of the effect be deduced from those of the cause? No. True, they are "grounded" in the latter, but they cannot be deduced them. Qualities cannot be derived. Quality comes first. And it is seen, grasped, established.

Does that mean that the appearance of the quality does not have a sufficient reason? By no means. The sufficient reason exists; it consists of the qualities of the cause. But the manner of the qualitative relationship of effect to cause is different from the quantitative. It is that of appearance. This means more than juxtaposition. If I compare the properties of the effect and of the cause—for example, steam with its specific determinations; then water; then the heat created by combustion—I then grasp a meaningful whole, namely, the issuance of the effect from the cause. I grasp the individual determinants of this whole as having a meaningful bearing to one another. It is a relationship of properties, an essential relationship. I can and ought to comprehend, penetrate and understand it as true. Thereby I acquire the certainty of evidence. I am standing on solid ground. But I cannot make a derivation.

In the realm of the qualitative, therefore, the law of sufficient reason takes on a different form than in the quantitative. How does it differ? Recognition of the sufficient reason is present. It lies in the evidence by which I grasp the qualitative relationship existing between the properties of the effect and those of the cause. But the effect cannot be derived from the cause. It can only be accepted and then comprehended.

Let us consider the animate sphere of existence. We shall group together the biological animate and the psychological animate.

The animate has its quantities—the sum total of what can be measured. It possesses its relationships of quality, namely, the chemistry and physics of the animate. Over and above that, however, it possesses qualities proper to itself and a proper manner in which these qualities become actual, quite different from those of the inanimate.

Vital processes are extremely varied. We can reduce them to three: the process of origin, of perpetuation; the process of preservation and of growth; the process of locomotion in the wider sense of the word.

Do these vital processes have their sufficient reason? Certainly. Where does it lie? Not in the quantitative element. That point has already been established with regard to the inanimate. It does not lie in the qualitative relationships of the inanimate either. Life never comes from non-life. Where then? Only in the animate itself. The proposition that life can originate from non-life is not a scientific view, but a working hypothesis, posed in order to derive everything possible from chemical and mechanical research. Furthermore, it is a dogma, but a very questionable one. Life comes only from life. The sufficient reason for this animate is the animate itself. And the manner in which this sufficient reason becomes active is likewise proper to itself— propagation, growth and locomotion.

We have seen that the magnitude of the effect can be derived, penetrated, confirmed and projected from the magnitude of the cause. The effect, the procession of the qualities of the effect, could not be derived from the qualitative cause in the realm of the inanimate. The effect had the character of otherness, of novelty. The new quality "appeared." It demanded of the observer an attitude, a special capacity to see this underivable appearance and to accept it. In his day Sombart defined the mechanical and economical attitude of the bourgeois type as calculating. The bourgeois mentality can only exist if it possesses calculable certainty. It feels safe only to the extent of its calculations. The bourgeois is a quantitative man who finds assurance of existence solely in derivable relationships of quantity. Opposed to him, we ought to continue, we find the qualitative man, who is a man of both daring and trust. He is capable of accompanying the "leap" which quality of effect makes from quality of cause; he finds the non-calculable relationships of essence and form more trustworthy and sustaining than the relationships of calculation.

This element becomes more complicated in the area of the animate. Impenetrability increases. The relationship of qualitative change in the inanimate realm had the character of rigid, uniform constancy. In the realm of the animate not only is it calculably impossible to see how the quality of the effect proceeds from the cause, but there is the added consideration of elasticity. Unpredictability does not cease even when the typical structure is recognized. When all the active causes, qualitative as well as quantitative, have been definitely determined, then the result of complex chemical and physical causes is likewise determined univocally. On the contrary, no matter how well the properties of a plant are known, no matter how exactly all the requirements for an experiment on it are determined, the possibility of surprise always remains, making the result unpredictable. This does not come about by reason of the complexity of the requirements, but because these requirements harbor a special, essentially incalculable factor. It consists precisely in the particular manner of vital function. The animate is essentially individual and productive. Once the product is present, it can be evaluated in its complete and meaningful relationship with its presuppositions. namely, in its relationship of production, as the form of the specific, qualitative category of a living being.

Now we shall mount to another sphere, the realm of the spiritual. By it I understand those acts that implicate being and meaning, that take a position, evaluate and decide, that realize values—and that which supports those acts.

In the first place, there is the act of knowledge. It too includes a quantitative element; experimental psychology seeks to grasp it. The act also includes biological and psychological elements. Beyond that there is something new, namely, the process of knowledge in the strict sense: the fact that I comprehend the object, its essence, its value, its meaning; that I am enlightened; that I understand and judge; that I gain truth. This is something *sui generis*.

Does this process have its sufficient reason? Undoubtedly! Where does it ultimately lie? Solely and exclusively in the living, spiritual power of comprehension itself. It resides in what the ancient philosophy called "the truth of the thing"; in the objective character inherent in existence itself that is recognizable and begets knowledge.

How does this sufficient reason function? How does knowledge proceed from its sufficient reason? Not by derivation of the quantitative relationships; not with the necessity and constancy of physical and chemical laws; neither in the manner of a bio-physiological function of the organ or of one phase of growth from another, but—as a spiritual act from a living spirit. Here we have a new qualitative category. It can only be ascertained and accepted.

The element of incalculability has risen enormously; so, too, the element of productivity. This has received a new character, that of formation and creation. In both a new extent and significance the attitude of acceptance, of openness, of reverence for the creative power of the spirit is demanded—an attitude that does not seek to examine and verify, but accepts. It is capable of perceiving that with every spiritual creation a world such as does not yet exist in simple nature comes into being; it becomes so only by reason of creative spiritual acts. With regard to these acts and their product another kind of acceptance and penetration is demanded—understanding.

The same holds true of the genesis of the work of art from the creative artist, of the origin of decisive action, of the establishment of order, and so forth.

In a particular manner this phenomenon manifests itself in the most intimate province of the spiritual, namely, in personal life, for example, in an act of gratitude or of love. Here all the forms of the law of sufficient reason hitherto mentioned come into play, for the person is a real person. Now, personal acts are accomplished not in some vague transcendental sphere, but in the real order. Here are real acts of the real person, and everything pertaining to human reality enters into these acts. To the realistic realms, however, of the psychic, of the biological-physical and of the axiological, something new is added: the self-enrichment and self-preservation of the living, spiritual person; the actualization of personal relationships with their supporters, as in friendship, marriage, comradeship, offspring, and the like.

Do these acts and relationships possess their sufficient reason? But let us not put the question so generally. We shall instead inquire into a concretely experienced personal bond. Do I experience a real friendship as sufficiently established? Most certainly. Less sufficiently, less solidly established than a mathematical relationship or biological causality? On the contrary! It is more solid, stronger. Solid in a new and different manner. The absoluteness of the axioms of quantities guarantees the mathematical relationship; the validity of the qualitative structure assures the biological relationship, and so on. The specific assurance which lies in the participation of the person guarantees the personal relationship. Every genuine personal relationship is experienced as freely placed. At the same time it experiences a peculiar necessity, namely, that it is "right," that it cannot be otherwise. Here, naturally, we have a very different necessity, a personal one. Every genuine personal relationship finds its ultimate basis in itself. Plato's myth about man who was split asunder, whose two halves now seek one another so that whenever persons tend toward one another those separated halves of the whole man work toward unity in them—this myth gives metaphysical expression to the consciousness of a most profound "foundation." But in our present context, this foundation works in a different manner—that in which a personal and spiritual

9

being disposes of itself, preserves and gives away itself, remains isolated or creates a relationship with another.

If I wish to understand this basis fully, I can do so only by assuming the required attitude. I must renounce calculation and re-examination. Indeed, even psychological or sociological analysis must at a certain point be sacrificed. I must deal only with the meaning proceeding from personal disposition, consider the unique relation of one thing to another.

Now we are face to face with freedom.

As soon as a free action is performed a qualitatively new sphere of events comes into being. All the forms of the law of "sufficient reason," as hitherto explained, return to it. For the free action is a real action. It does not happen in an intelligible sphere outside the real. It is real, borne by a real subject, the concrete person. This concrete person, with all his being, shares in it. But beyond the various forms described thus far, the free action contains something new, precisely the fact that it is free. The manner in which the free process goes forth from its sufficient reason is the manner of the act.

The element of calculating penetrability is reduced here to a minimum. Strictly speaking, the free action excludes all calculation. If any reckoning is made, it will concern itself with the question as to whether the action is really free or whether a greater or lesser degree of habit exists in it. On the other hand, the specific certainty found in it has its own character. It represents confidence in the intention, confidence in the fact that the one performing the free action has assumed the moral law into his freedom. But this assurance is of an entirely different kind from that produced by conformity to mathematical, biological or psychological laws. It has nothing to do with calculable derivation. As a matter of fact, it is destroyed by such derivation. If an architect builds a bridge, if an advertiser promotes a venture, if a leader organizes a union, they build on the assurance of statistical, mass-psychological and economic laws. But if there is question of the given promise being freely maintained, then those laws touch only the periphery of the free-trustworthy action. Its core is touched solely by the confidence, that is, the belief, that the other party has assumed the moral law, the law of honesty, into his innermost being. Thereby the initiative itself is "assured," so free as to exclude all possibility of coercion. As soon, however, as I would give psychological or economical assurance to the other party that I was reckoning with, I would basically destroy the attitude of trust, and he would have the right to spurn me angrily.

The element of originality, of production, here reaches its apogee. Freedom is simply the human creative act. *"Sub Deo omnipotentia—*Omnipotence under God," St. Anselm calls it. Alone suitable to it is that form of comprehension which is borne along by reverence in the strict sense, as the attitude demanded by freedom and its sovereignty.

We have now exhausted the fields existing in this world. But the thread of meaning that runs through them continues farther. True, not in the sense of a direct connection, but in that form which the ancient philosophy called analogy: similarity, though a basic difference exists.

Thus we arrive at God's realm.

The divine act possesses a new quality; it is absolute. Such absoluteness signifies not only the summit, but also a new property, namely, the property of God. In our discussion it means the immediate production of the effect by the cause with no prerequisite either of material or of model or of design. God is archetype, creative reason and final goal. In the case of the creature, the question of sufficient reason always implies that the process under consideration is subject to a law and asks to what extent it is subject. God, however, is subject to no law. He is simply the law—and by nature he is also simply freedom. Our minds cannot grasp how these two elements are integrated in one Being. "Sufficient reason," of which we have spoken hitherto, is a determined human conceptual form of the fact that God exists, that the world is his creation and, as such, a reflection of him. The attitude owed to him is that of absolute reverence, that is, of adoration. To attempt any derivation here is not only absurd, but also religiously objectionable, sacrilege. We must not think "beyond God," but begin with God, for he is absolute origin. He is not derived.

Revelation opens a qualitatively new sphere. It forms the realm of substantial mystery. It remains hidden to the extent that it does not reveal itself; it still remains impenetrable. Here, too, everything that happens has its sufficient reason. But the manner in which things proceed from it is proper to itself. It is primarily and basically the manner of God's own inner life. The all-governing majesty of the Father possesses it *simpliciter*. Eternally the Son proceeds from him by generation and by expression of the paternal word. From both comes the Holy Spirit in the breath of love. Applied to man, it is the manner of grace, in which the love of God, through the mystery of rebirth, grants likeness and participation in his own life.

Here impenetrability is absolute. The act by which we enter into this realm and move about in it is faith, which in its turn comes from God.

The critical manifestation of this impenetrability, which likewise and by reason of God's free grace finds its full and sufficient reason, is the miracle.

From what has been said, a unique concatenation of ideas emerges.

Reality—I mean reality as it exists, not as something

vaguely conceived—has a twofold aspect: the quantitative
aspect of measurability and the quantitative aspect of
definite determination. The quantitative element permeates
the various realms of reality. But it loses significance as the
order of the realm of being rises. In God, absoluteness
swallows up all measure; in the realm of revelation, grace
swallows up all calculation and all pretension. In the same
manner the qualitative element passes through the various
realms of reality. Progressively the consideration of more or
less loses importance, while that of thus or otherwise gains in
importance. Indeed, God's absoluteness is also his measure;
but it is a name. And the glowing of the heart of Jesus
weighs "as much" as the mass of all sins.

Now, as far as our question is concerned, this means that
the more exalted the realms in the order of the real, the less
important the significance of derivation and the greater the
degree of originality.

We spoke of the appearance of quality in the inanimate
creation; of the productiveness in the animate creation; of
formative, creative activity and of personal self-determina-
tion in the realm of the spirit; of freedom in the field of
moral action. Then, above that, in God's realm, to be
attained *per analogiam,* of absolute creation; and in the field
of revelation, of the triune life of God and of grace. With
each step the character of the productive element grew, in
contradistinction to the dispositive, to simple distribution
and arrangement. And while the quantitative element had
its place with regard to investigation and derivation, exact
demonstration, the increasing importance of the qualitative
element demands an attitude of acceptance, of openness, of
trust, of daring—to the field of faith.

Both elements, the quantitative with its derivability, and
the qualitative with its graded originality, belong in the
world.

The attempt is made to explain the world only by the first. Its result is a quantitative and mechanistic view of the world. It does not prove, but rests on a presupposition. It bears within itself a model image, a determined concept of the perfect. Using this as a basis, it asserts, compares, judges and decides. This is the perfection of exact penetration: formula and machine. No place is given to anything that spells originality. Underivable processes are not only impossible, but meaningless, ugly, worthless. They are a wrench thrown into the machinery. They contradict the determinative element here, namely, calculability. Quality and its appearance already are impossible. Everything qualitative is converted into quantity. Progressively vital production, spiritual creation and especially the free act become "more impossible," more insupportable—not to speak of God's activity and the miracle of grace. On every plane the proper element is explained mechanistically.

On the other hand, the attempt is likewise made to grasp the world purely from the qualitative side. Therefrom emerge the primitive, the magical, the romantic and the purely religious images of the world. The determinative concepts in this case are quite different: living organism; harmony of elements of a qualitative nature; field of opposing powers; spheres of eternal production. The "world" here is always the product of creative, opposing, harmonious powers. In this world there is no room for anything that smacks of exact, derivable necessity. Everything remains in flux, continues in the hand of creative might. Anything always remains possible. Beside every "law," even the most incisive, stands the possibility of abrogation. Ultimately even law has not the significance of exact definition, but of symbolic expression and of musical harmony (consider the mathematical magic of Novalis). Basically everything is a miracle. The normal does not exist.

The first image ends in the frenzy of the world-machine; the latter in the fantasy of a cosmic play or cosmic struggle. The real world embraces both of these.

Moreover, the real world exists in such a manner that these separate concepts are considered as one.

In this world freedom plays a role. This world exists in such a manner that freedom has a path prepared for itself. The first decision whether freedom is acknowledged or denied has to do fundamentally with the question of whether or not one admits quality in contradistinction to quantity. The world exists in such a way that step by step it prepares itself for freedom and is completed only by the free act.

Whenever, therefore, a man acts with freedom, the world takes its final step.

Living Spirit

I

The preceding investigation dealt with freedom. But the question remains as to how such freedom is possible. Despite all the preparation based on the general presuppositions of being, the following question demands an answer: How is a mode of activity possible which in the general picture is so self-sufficient as free action?

We then spoke of the immutable: how immutability in its various forms is experienced and mastered by man; how freedom finds its place in the order of necessity. Here, too, the question remained open. The relation in which free man stands to immutability is different from the manner in which a stone rolls or a tree grows. His relationship to the immutable has a specific quality, cheek by jowl with that of freedom. This form of immutability is related to freedom; one presupposes the other. This holds true of that point which has to do with necessity in the profoundest depths of my being—that I exist and function in my innermost being so that I am able to assert, "I cannot do otherwise." This inability to act otherwise differs wholly from any kind of coercion; rather it coincides entirely with my most profound freedom. Hence there is question here of immutability of a unique kind. This special manner becomes possible by the fact that both freedom and the actuation of immutability are sustained by the spirit. To act in the manner called freedom and to exercise immutability in the particular manner in which we have described it is to manifest the spirit's being.

Now, what is spirit?

A few words have to be premised to the following explanation. The preceding investigations presented a direct concatenation of ideas. They started from a point of departure considered fruitful and proceeded step by step. The question that concerns us here calls for a different sort of investigation. The problem lies in the dialectical order, that is, it must be grasped simultaneously from various viewpoints. This will then also manifest itself in the exposition of ideas.

The second section attempts to show how the problem of the spirit appears in the purely philosophical light, that is, how the attempt of thought looks from this standpoint. Section III determines the point of view from which this question must be approached and sets up the thesis that this viewpoint can come about only through a specific relation of revelation and experience, of faith and natural thought processes. Section IV investigates the place of the spiritual element in experience. Section V looks for the point of departure, recognized as necessary, in faith. Section VI follows the path that has been prepared for it.

The reader is exhorted to think along each particular part of the investigation; to then break off and in like manner cooperate in the next part, keeping in mind, however, the conclusion of the preceding part; and, finally, to complete the last stretch on the basis of a multiple general plan.

If it is true that a man not only travels to attain a goal, but that the result already forms part of the movement toward the goal, then the completion of this dialectical mode of thought is not only a prerequisite for the result, but already to some extent the result itself.

II

The concept of spirit as manifested in ordinary as well as philosophical speech is multiple.

In the customary thought of the past decades, spirit signifies above all the sum total of objective meanings. Thus, for example, "science" as the relationship of queries, efforts at research and replies which the individual faces, which he accepts and carries on. Or "art," more exactly the relationship of artistic activity; or "State," as the realization of the concept of law, and so on. Here spirit at the same time connotes a cultural attitude—the objective spirit. This holds true of the idealistic tradition.

The same tradition also understands by spirit the sum total of those prerequisites that bring about such culture or are necessary to comprehend it. This includes the prerequisites of thought: the subject, the categories, the laws of logic; the prerequisites of the artistic act, of creative activity and of understanding: the structures of meaning and of the function of the esthetic act; the fact of law and the rule of law as prerequisites for social order, and so on. Spirit, in this sense, is consequently the subject of culture and of its categorical structure, as opposed to the schema of culture, the object of culture.

Earlier thought, with excellent justification, emphasized the element of being. Spirit is immaterial existence; not a composite substance, but simple and therefore indestructible, imperishable, independent of matter. If the two previously described concepts portrayed an inclination to view spirit as something abstract, as something logical or at least formal, the present concept brings with it the danger or the possibility of neutralizing the spirit, of considering it a higher piece of natural reality—the danger of overlooking the content of spiritual existence, of bypassing the fact that spiritual existence also means fulfillment of duties, realization of what ought to be, putting all the weight on the sustaining substance. This view prevails in the Gnostic-dualistic philosophy with all its ramifications.

By way of contrast, we have the actualistic concept, deriving today particularly from Kierkegaard and from phenomenological dynamism. This looks upon spirit not as something that exists but always as something that is done, or rather, as something that happens. More precisely, spirit is a "relationship," a manner in which man looks at himself. Spirit comes into existence when man assumes responsibility for himself. To be conscious of himself, to assume responsibility for himself, to take an attitude toward what a person is and ought to be—that is spirit for the actualist.

Thus a manifold danger threatens the clarity of the concept of spirit as regards its point of departure. First, spirit appears as "the content of culture"; then as logic; then again as a piece of reality, existing in its own way as a mineral or a plant exists in its fashion; finally, strictly considered, it becomes a borderline situation, actual only transiently and by approximation.

Other significations of the word and of the concept might be traced. There is the great antithesis of the Romantic concept of spirit: spirit is light, an airy lightness; a dangerous—but exhilaratingly dangerous—climax of existence; the sustaining, governing, active element in everything. In the last analysis, spirit and genius are equated. At the same time, however, spirit is regarded as a disturbing element in life, as destroying intimacy, undermining all security, as that which uproots, empties and overthrows—a concept of spirit which for Nietzsche and his disciples, for Bachofen, for Klages and others becomes the sum total of evil.

Spirit may signify the living content of being, as when we speak of the "medieval spirit," of the "martial spirit," or of the "spirit of St. Benedict."

It may signify, too, the suprarational, living wave of energy and content that waxes and wanes, as in the expression, "The inhabitants of Umbria were seized by the Franciscan spirit." In this instance it becomes a manifestation of community life.

In all these formulations, a true aspect of that mysterious something comes to the fore. But an aspect does not see itself; a concept does not think itself. Only living living man sees and thinks, and he is always prejudiced. Then it appears that the gaze wanders, that the movement of thought runs imperceptibly into an impossibility, into a contradiction. As a result, one begins to wonder if it is possible at all, by a simple consideration of internal and external data, by a simple analysis, by a logical process of thought, to grasp something like spirit in its essence. The abstract ability of recognition may indeed be present, but the concrete is lacking. Objective data may be at hand, and still the concept may be substantially vitiated.

III

We get to firm ground only by a question that probes deeper. Do the various objects of my knowledge reach me in the same manner?

No. There are various ways, more particularly three, by which something comes into my possession.

First there is the "natural" way that opens me to the sum total of objects in the realm of the world, the realities, both external and internal that are attainable by me as man and the ideas, values, meanings, categories, logical forms, and so on that become understandable from or by these realities.

In contrast to this, there is the "supernatural" way. This does not imply any abnormal, pathological phenomena. Nor does it imply—though they may be possible—such supranormal abilities as clairvoyance. Instead, we are dealing here with realities, values, ideas, relationships, and so on that do not belong to the "world" in the ordinary sense, but which become our property only by a special and clearly marked process called revelation.

The first point which differentiates revelation from a generic religious process of expression is the assertion that God speaks. The prophet intones, "Thus says the Lord . . ." Christ, sent by the Father, proclaims, "I tell you . . ."

Now, how does the content of the divine declaration become the property of the hearer? How does it become credible and comprehensible?

In the process of revelation we may distinguish the means and the significance of the revelation. The former consists of things, powers, procedures, data of the internal and external field of experience—the material of experience in general, that which takes place in us and around us.

In revelation, however, it happens that this particular

process, behavior, figure, action, human thought, and so on, while they are data belonging to the world, nevertheless awaken the impression that there is something else, not earthly. The material of this world clearly points to something that does not belong to the world. And this not in the form of a purely subjective feeling, but as the perception of objective data. Not in the sense, therefore, that the individual in question alone is personally involved so that he is justified in declaring that what is asserted has this or that meaning for him. But so that truth obliges him to state: Now, this is really something! The person who is presented, his appearance and actions, his words and thoughts all point to things not belonging to this earth but to heaven, to that which comes "from above." After Christ has spoken his hearers remark, "He speaks like one having authority." They perceive this authority, definitely not of this world, which "the scribes and pharisees" do not possess, from his physical, biological, psychological manner of speaking, accommodated to the texture of the world. They intend to throw him from a precipice at Nazareth. "But he, passing through their midst, went his way." This action performed before their eyes, his attitude, bespeak something that roots them to the spot. Discussing the cleansing of the Temple, Jerome remarks, "Something ethereal emanated from his brow."

Revelation signifies something further; in fact, it is implied in what has already been said. In the words, in the gestures, in the living being of the revealing person something strikes the individual who is ready to believe as a content that patently is not of this world. It is not only that mundane elements produce a supramundane impression, but a supramundane content clearly comes to the fore. Christ has spoken of the Father. Philip says, "Lord, show us the Father and it is enough for us." He replies, "Have I been so long a time with you, and you have not known me?

Philip, he who sees me sees also the Father." Here, too, belong the words of John's first epistle: "I write of what was from the beginning, what we have heard, what we have seen with our eyes, what we have looked upon and our hands have handled: of the Word of Life. And the Life was made known which was with the Father, and has appeared to us." His gospel similarly says, "We saw his glory—glory as of the only-begotten of the Father." Substantial divine glory becomes visible in him; he who wills can see it.

"To be a man" does not mean that the spiritual soul takes up residence in a preformed body, but that it fashions a body. "Body" already implies soul, a soul expressing itself. To this corresponds—though on an absolutely more exalted and different basis—the inner relationship of the divine-human existence. The Son of God did not simply dwell in a human nature, but he "became man"—the God-man. His human substance from its very first moment excels our purely human substance; it is divine and human, a manifestation "of the glory of the only-begotten of the Father," so that "he who sees him sees the Father." Precisely about this point, in which the mystery of the incarnation centers, raged the whole Nestorian controversy.

When Jesus speaks of love, when he proposes the order of love and himself lives it, then we not only behold an expression of something unknown and exalted in recognizable form, but we perceive something new and distinct. Mundane words, mundane experiences are employed in such a manner that through them, thanks to the analogical power of created being and thought, higher realities are expressed. When Jesus speaks of "love," it is qualitatively different from love as discussed psychologically or ethically on the basis of human experience. Still the data of experience are employed in such a way that it becomes clear to the believer *in lumine fidei* that analogically they signify more than the naturally experienceable.

Thus far we have discussed the manifestation of revelation. It is taken up by faith. Now, faith is a proper, autonomous act. It does not represent a dilution of or even a prelude to knowledge, nor does it serve solely as a means of communicating knowledge. Faith is something *sui generis,* both psychologically and metaphysically. Faith itself is supernatural. It proceeds from the same source as revelation. It is an act granted by God. It is one of the "theological" virtues. By faith we are enabled, with the assistance of grace, to share in the power by which God knows his own essence. The paradox expressed by Gregory the Great contains deep meaning: to believe does not mean so much that we recognize God as that we are recognized by God. In this mystery of faith, the psychological act of believing constitutes, as it were, the body, the mundane, experienceable actuation.

The act of faith is related to revelation as mundane experience and thought are to a mundane datum. Believing is the act whereby the person who is prepared, who opens himself to grace, "who has eyes to see," sees, and "who has ears to hear," hears; the act whereby he grasps the "otherworldly" in the mundane, perceives the more exalted content, understands the higher reality from the proclaiming, witnessing word.

World and perception of the world; revelation and faith—these are two forms of data and understanding of data. But there is a third, and it is here that the problem that particularly confronts us lies.

What I am now about to present imposed itself on me in the course of long and hard cogitation. I still cannot sufficiently prove it; nevertheless I should like to be allowed to present it as a working hypothesis, with the hope that it will prove its worth by its fruits. I am convinced that it fits in with the great religious philosophies of the past no less than with the direction of the expected development of contemporary religious thinking.

Certain realities, values, demands, relationships belong to this world. Strictly speaking, they pertain to me as man, to the realm of experience and thought readily accessible to me. Theoretically, therefore, these things would have to represent complete, purely natural data. Actually, however, it rarely comes to that. More often it occurs either not at all, so that they remain entirely in the dark, or indistinctly, only by approximation, so that they cannot be clearly defined—a form of elusiveness in which the intended sense is grasped and then again escapes. It would seem that the object is veiled, displaced by other objects; something noble and delicate by what is more crude; something complicated, demanding greater effort on the part of the intellect, by what is more obvious, easier to understand.

Objects demand a varying degree of application for their understanding. Our process of thought, as a biological and psychological act, operates under the principle of minimum expenditure of energy. Thus this delicate technique plays with the tendency to overlook data that demand greater concentration or to accommodate itself to those that can be grasped more readily. More exalted objects not only call for a greater application of intellectual power, but a qualitatively different approach. The entire problem of ethics and of cultural doctrine lies here, in the question of "the existentiality of thought." Just as surely as thought differs from existence in the understanding of objective reality, so this objective understanding of reality cannot be dissociated from the concrete being of the thinker. The limitation of this phase of the problem can be expressed by the proposition: Really I know only what I am, at the least that on which I engage myself. That holds true particularly of objects that affect me, that have to do with my human, moral personal existence. The more exalted the fact, the less possibility of perceiving it simply because a greater degree of self-hazard is required. An automatically functioning technique of veiling, of pushing back, of undermining, of emptying, is led on by the mute will of the personality trying to defend itself—the personality which refuses to take a chance, which wants "to preserve itself," and hence desires that the facts in question should not exist. As a result, these facts are not considered at all or only partially and obliquely.

The facts in our case are actually the highest in the natural realm, pertaining to the uppermost category of value; the most delicate; the most complicated; of supreme significance for our personal well-being. Trying to understand them makes gigantic demands on the intellect. They seriously threaten the smooth, rational, well-ordered world-picture by offering insoluble problems that demand of existential thinking the supreme commitment of the ego.

We are speaking of spiritual and personal facts: God, and indeed the real God, not only the "Absolute," or the concept of some other kind of "ultimate" person, the living person, not just the logical subject or the psychological center of activity; spirit, and again, the living spirit. We must also include everything related to these facts as values, demands, or orders: freedom; love; the various essential forms of human and personal relationship like marriage, friendship, country; the basic phenomena of history, for example, the various forms of personal contact, activity, decision and the like. It represents that realm in which lie the problems of our proper, human existence and in which the judgment regarding this existence is pronounced.

Now, it appears to me that history as well as personal experience and observation show that these personal

10

realities, demands and orders, which *per se* belong to the realm of nature, cannot be sufficiently explained on the basis of that realm. They do not emerge clearly. They cannot be quietly analyzed. Natural understanding does not grasp their essence purely, their contour clearly, their content whole and entire. They stand off in the distance. They are veiled. Our understanding finds them elusive. Again and again they are immersed in and sucked down by their environment. Similarities appear and are confused with them, for example, "person" with "individual" or with "subject" or—most subtle of errors—with "personality."

If they are to come to the fore completely and distinctly, if they are to be analyzed so that the intellect can clearly grasp them and the will make a decision regarding them, then they have to be liberated and secured by a corresponding revelation of content. Not self-revealed—the content of revelation is that which comes "from above," which is "not of this world"—but pointed up by corresponding truths of revelation which offer an analogy to them.

Full perception of "person," the real, genuine person, can be had only when it becomes clear by revelation and is grasped by faith what the child of God is. "Person" signifies something else than "child of God." The former is a natural reality, the latter belongs to the supernatural, pneumatic order. "Child of God" signifies something that man is by grace, by redemption; "person," what he is by birth. But what constitutes a "person," an independent person, in contrast to organic and esthetic personality; a concrete person, in contrast to the sociological organism and the element of historical development; a person capable of order and obligation and full responsibility, in contrast to the utopian notion of a self-sufficient being; a person with self-identity, which can be addressed, which in the profoundest sense can be an object, in contrast to the mere glow of a dynamic act; a person illuminating and responsible for the entire wealth of the human being and of human life, in contrast to a mere juridical ascription of responsibility and ownership? These contrasts are not purely fabricated possibilities, but *de facto* again and again the genuine concept of person is destroyed by the failure to see them. All this and more becomes evident, is clearly grasped, remains assured only when faith, based on revelation, accepts the religious reality of divine filiation: namely, that man, by reason of God's creative love, becomes a child of God; that, by the same token, he becomes an object of absolute value, that is, of God's affection, creatively established by God as an object of his divine love; a bearer of infinite treasure, namely, the blood of Christ; destined solely for God, his Father, of whom he may say, "God and my soul—nothing else exists on earth"; engrafted into the sum total of God's kingdom and entitled to take a familiar attitude with regard to God—to say, "our Father." His attitude is that of humility which makes him conscious of the fact that he lives wholly by grace, that he is not sovereign and self-sufficient. At the same time he knows that he is responsible for a decision concerning weal or woe that carries over into eternity. He has been told that "it avails him nothing to gain the whole world if he suffers the loss of his own soul."

At the same time his lot in this world is indicated. He is told to give "to Caesar what belongs to Caesar"; uprightly to love his neighbor as himself. All this forms the content of the revelation of divine filiation. It is not drawn from his own thought processes or from the consideration of his own dignity, but announced in the word of the glad tidings, expressed in the living attitude of Christ, developed in the New Testament. If this is grasped by faith and realized in vital activity; if at least a readiness for it becomes apparent, then in its light will shine forth that reality which has its counterpart in the natural sphere and which furnishes the natural substratum—the person.

The meaning of conscience—responsibility with all its implications and its limits, human responsibility not that of a divinely sovereign being, but yet human responsibility as differentiated from animal behavior or the simple influence of environment—this will make it apparent, if it becomes apparent at all, that man's eternal salvation stems wholly from God, that it is a gift and a grace, and yet that it has to be worked out "with fear and trembling."

History, as something distinct from biologically causal development or random occurrence, really becomes clear only from revelation. There we discover what it means that God enters into time, and how consequently, by means of a salvific event, sacred history is constituted. This event looks back to the divine act of the creation of the world and gazes ahead to the last judgment. The whole is borne along by God's providence and man's decision.

The genuine meaning of the "State"—neither an "all-pervading god" nor yet a "cold monster"; neither a simple idea nor a security mechanism—only becomes evident when revelation shows us the significance of the kingdom of God.

Much more might be said on this subject.

What I shall now state appears like a monstrous heresy in the light of the doctrine of autonomy proposed in recent times, and yet everything seems to me to point to this one conclusion: there is no such thing as completely independent knowledge of matters pertaining to the realm of the personal and the spiritual.

The objects of this realm are natural. Strictly speaking, they pertain to the fields of philosophy, psychology, sociology, and so forth. But they attain univocal and complete meaning only when their analogous supernatural realities are presented by revelation and grasped by faith. They are apprehended clearly only as long as this faith persists. The clarity of these objects increases and diminishes with the intensity and clarity of the life of faith. As soon as faith disappears they sink back into a characteristic twilight, recede and escape. Striking examples of this sort of thing can be adduced from our own times.

The foregoing contains a decision. It implies a fundamental break with the naïve assurance of idealistic thinking. Indeed, it goes farther. It applies not only to knowledge but also to taking a position, to activity. Here it signifies a rejection of the modern demand for an autonomous culture. There is no autonomous culture, assuming that "culture" demands that it rise above the realm of knowledge supplied by the natural sciences, the utilitarian aspect of economic and social studies, the lower rungs of artistic education. As soon as culture is taken to mean struggle in the realm of the spiritual and personal in order thus to permeate the whole of existence, the self-evident manner in which the question of an autonomous culture is treated today becomes naïveté. Either there is no such thing as revelation, and then we have no other recourse but to be satisfied with a perpetual change of viewpoint, with an eternal happenstance, or, on the contrary, we recognize the reality and the meaning of the fact of revelation as well as the longing of the natural life of the spirit for revelation, and then the peculiar situation we have adumbrated becomes clear. Genuine progress to real values is possible, but only from the vantage point of faith. Naturally, this can be taken neither in the sense of religious traditionalism nor of a theocracy of culture. It may not signify either that cultural works produce their fruit without effort. Revelation and faith detract nothing from natural labor. The entire task of drawing the marrow from the data of the world by human thought and action remains. Absolute autonomy of cultural work is destroyed; a relative autonomy, however, remains. Religious sentiment has a tendency to go immediately to the last step in all things, to take cognizance of the ultimate as the solution of the problem and to want to see in the will to attain that ultimate the fulfillment of the task. Herein lies the specific danger of the religious attitude. It would destroy culture; it would rob natural activity of its responsibility and joyousness. If absolute autonomy has been proved fallacious, if it has been shown that only in the light of revelation can the world be viewed aright, then with might and main the relative autonomy of the world's task must be sustained.

IV

Now we have taken position.

It behooves us to direct the inner eye, the ability to perceive the essential, to the point where "spirit" is, to the point where spirit manifests itself as something special, qualitatively characteristic.

Let us observe a man's approach to a problem. He works his way through the confusion of facts, the network of relations, the multiplicity of divergent ways. At first the congeries of the factual is chaos to him, but gradually order proceeds from the point of departure of the question. The question casts doubt on what hitherto seemed secure, but by the intrinsic indifference of genuine inquiry the questioner remains above the doubtful, and by the process of deep delving he establishes a new basis, until finally the meaningful element comes to light—the spirit.

Man stands in the midst of the stuff of life. Relationships, duties, an experience, a tragedy or whatever it may be —these things pile upon him. He takes hold, and by the power of transformation he conquers. At first all is heavy, burdensome. He lifts from within. He makes the burden light, His existence is deeply rooted in suffering, but it rises in clarity and lightness. It acquires the ability to move freely.

This is a labor of ascent, of human, moral, artistic lightness. Spirit is there.

A man receives an idea, a problem, into his innermost being. He has assumed it entirely into himself, dedicated himself entirely to it. And now he struggles and labors. It seems as if there were in him a flame that sucks in and consumes his life. He feeds it piece after piece of his existence. To all appearances he impoverishes his life. He suffers excruciatingly under this continuous sacrifice; but he knows that everything depends on that one glowing point. Call to mind a man like Francis or—thought entirely different—a man like Kierkegaard. Give up everything! Withhold nothing! All the goods of health, of harmony, of happiness, of culture lose their significance. And yet the man realizes that in the complete sacrifice he finds fulfillment, the one thing that counts. Spirit is there.

Here we have a man with specific, clearly discernible talents. The reckoning of his powers can readily be made. If you are acquainted with him, you know his character, his possibilities, you can almost foretell the course his development will take. This man does his work; he concerns himself about right and justice; he lives his life. But in his innermost being dwells the mystery of readiness, and throughout everything he does and consciously wills a transformation proceeding from within takes place. Something there is that makes him receptive to things that hitherto had been closed to him. Beyond all calculable psychological possibilities he becomes steadily enlarged, richer, finer and better. A gradual transformation takes place—so quiet that he himself is not aware of it; possibly only a friend, on occasion as it were confronted with the comparison, perceives what has occurred. Everything takes on depth, transparency, illuminating power. The transformation affects even his countenance, his tone of voice. Spirit is there.

One man knows another, is intimately acquainted with him. In his heart of hearts he has assented to him, has assumed the other's name into himself—and truly at times a person knows the name of another better than his own. Now he bears this characteristic thing in himself, alert and steady, without deviation. Here we have vital activity. He keeps the essence of the other in his heart. He sees clearly, even if everything becomes blurred for the other. By the clairvoyance of love, he perceives how everything is and how everything ought to be. He keeps the essential image upright, even though the other may allow it to falter. He demands— not as self-seeking demands, but as love does—and demands inexorably that the other become the man he ought to be. And this he carries through, not by way of romances and dreams and exaggerations, but through the whole of workaday life, whether present or absent, *hieme et aestate, prope et procul, usquedem et ultra.* This power conquers. The other becomes what he ought to be. Spirit is there.

A man lives his daily life. The stream of events, of habit, again and again, at times in a new fashion, converges into something which we call a situation—a characteristic conjunction of happenings, things that advance or hinder, motives and impulses, pros and cons, restlessness and uncertainty. We have here a section of the stream of events, and yet it is as self-contained as a circle which looks outward from its center, and the center lies in the conscience of the individual. Everything is flowing, but here something stands immovable—the point of meaning, the question, the challenge. The man understands this, perceives it and stands firm —and that can happen in the smoothest, simplest manner, without any special reflection. He forges ahead to that quiet nucleus, passing unperturbed through the raging whirlpool of life and of events. He understands the situation; he perceives the voice of duty; he obeys, decides, and the stream goes on its way as if nothing had happened. But in truth this human existence—and with it also the existence of the world —have again received their meaning, even if no one else has perceived anything of it all. Spirit is there.

Much more might be mentioned in the same vein: the effect for weal or woe of the living thought; the productive power of the genuinely constructed personality, of example; form, rule and order proceeding from a vital ordaining power . . . All of these manifest the living spirit.

But—what is that living spirit?

V

We learn definitively what the genuine natural spirit is as soon as, by a living act of faith, we grasp from the revealing personality and its word what the Holy Spirit signifies and what he produces, namely, the spiritual. The *pneuma hagion* is at the same time the field of action and the guarantor of the natural spirit and of the natural-spiritual sphere.

The Holy Spirit hovers about the revealing personality. The Holy Spirit is Christ's habitat; he comes forth from him—mysterious, inscrutable. Christ speaks of those who are "born of the Spirit," puzzling to all others, like the wind that blows, no one knows whence. He was conceived by the Holy Spirit. At the baptism in the Jordan, the Holy Spirit descends upon him, drives him and guides him. The vibrant and vital element that weaves about the figure of Christ— that is he. One is almost tempted to say that is "it." He is called $Pν ε ῦμα \ ἅγιον$, a neuter: living breath, active power. It is he that turns the inner ear of the hearers to

Christ; that calls forth restlessness in the audience; that disturbs it and at the same time presages calm. Simultaneously he is "sword" and "peace." He brings it about that everything Christ is and says be understood as "not of this world," but as coming "from above," other-worldly, sacred, a breakthrough to God. "Sacred," primarily not in the ethical but in the religious sense: the reality of God which strikes us as foreign and yet as deeply intimate at the same time; which is to be feared, while simultaneously giving a sense of fulfillment, of a goal attained.

Christ appeals to the Holy Spirit. John reports the words, "Many things yet I have to say to you, but you cannot bear them now. But when he, the Spirit of truth, has come, he will teach you all truth." And precisely that truth with which we are concerned, the truth of Christ's revelation; he will make comprehensible what Christ has brought. "He will not speak on his own authority . . . He will receive of what is mine and declare it to you." For his own part, Christ is objective figure, expressed and permanent word, performed deed, accomplished suffering, offered sacrifice, established order. Man is confronted with all of this. During his lifetime Christ was not understood; people did not follow him. Pentecost saw the entrance of the Holy Spirit on the stage of history. He gave to men the power to comprehend what Christ was. He led men into "all truth." He brought home to them the revealing figure and its word and its redeeming act. Now they can understand. Now it can come about that Christ "remains in them and they in Christ"; that "they do not live, but Christ in them." Now begins the action of the productive word, the transforming deed, the unifying solidarity.

All of this happens in a personal relationship with God, as portrayed in and about Christ. "To be taught all truth"; "to have received what is Christ's," to understand the revela-

tion means to be child of the Father, disciple and brother
and sister of Christ, friend and client of the Holy Spirit, the
Paraclete.

That of which we spoke above, which appeared rather
nebulous, now assumes a univocal personal connotation. Not
only roaring wind and flame, not only "truth" and "love,"
but a person, a countenance that speaks and can be spoken
to—the "Friend," the Intercessor.

Paul has uttered most profound words about the Holy
Spirit: "Who among men knows the things of a man save
the spirit of the man that is in him? Even so, the things of
God no one knows but the Spirit of God." He "searches all
things, even the deep things of God." The Holy Spirit is
God's living inner disposition. God's sentiment. He
represents the manner in which God is present to his own
reality and truth—perfect belonging, unceasing penetration.
He illumines and consumes; he is perfectly pure and perfectly genuine, as representing absolute disposition. For this
reason he is completely and infinitely holy.

The faithful have been granted participation in this
Spirit. In the Holy Spirit we cry, "Abba! Father!" In him we
say "Lord Jesus." In the Spirit the believer must pray. In
him he must speak when the hour comes in which he is
called upon to witness to Christ.

As the bearer of this holy disposition the Christian must
live in the world—being not of the world, and yet in it. He
faces the unceasing turmoil of the world, which seeks to
draw everything into its sphere and to establish its
automony. The believer is perpetually exhorted to "overcome" the world, to construct the kingdom of God in it.

VI

The fact of the natural spirit appears in the environment

which this reality of revelation creates, in the holiness that emanates from it.

The critical and determinative point is the content of its life—to be more exact, the "critical" content, that is the sphere in which lies the spirit's obligatory performance and consequently, in the strict sense, the actuation of its essence. And here Augustine's dictum alone seems to fit: the essence of the created spirit is the *capacitas Dei,* the ability to comprehend God.

This is not a self-evident proposition, but rather something tremendous. Spirit is not self-evident. Here the whole of creation comes into focus.

Spirit is that reality by which man is able to comprehend God—as befits the nature of the creature, not in a manner proper to God, but by all those acts and ways in which man lays hold of God as an object, as a measure, as a prerequisite, within the limits defined by his human existence (the *status viatoris*); to comprehend God—not the absolute idea or the absolute value or simple absoluteness, but the real, living God. Spirit is that vital element in me which realizes its own full potential only when it has God for its content, as the content of its own life, in knowledge, in appreciation and decision, in formation and action.

We are speaking of the personal God, not of some generic world-being, not of some moving and operating world-reason. We mean the personal God who speaks and demands an answer. Spirit is that element in me than can be called upon by God, which really came into being by the fact that in the act of creation God called it; which bears a name, because in creation God named it. For the act by which it was created was an act of naming, of calling a thoroughly unique being. Thus spirit is that in me which henceforth will perceive God's call in everything that spells command and ordinance, and which can reply to such a call in a way of which it alone is capable.

By that fact spirit—and now I must say, my spirit and yours—has an immediate relationship to God. As living spirit it is not absorbed by the world. It does not simply belong to the world. Its contact with God is not by way of any worldly intermediary. Spirit comes directly from God. It is created by him as this unique being. Every spirit is created by God expressly and especially; named by God as this unique being, bearing a name that occurs only once. Thus it stands in immediate relationship to God. There is a mystery between it and God—a mystery indissoluble and direct.

Accordingly, my spirit is not enclosed in the created world. It does not come from the world and is not absorbed by it. And the world realizes this—even that "world" which I myself am. Spirit disturbs the world, agitates it. And yet the spirit works in the world. That is its field of duty. It has a mission to perform in the world—the mission to carry out the service of its calling.

This service is of such a nature that it can be accomplished only in the tension of being in the world and yet not of it. It works both by destruction and construction, not in the sense that a higher power of nature is here actuated —rising above psychological and sociological norms—but as personal perception of an appeal in conscience which realizes its responsibility to God, and judges, decides and operates on the basis of that responsibility with regard to things and events.

The Holy Spirit is the personal self-consciousness of God, in the love existing between the Father and the Son— somewhat like a *capacitas Dei ipsius*. Finite spirit is that creature which, by analogy applicable to creatures, has the ability to comprehend God, to attain him as the content of its life—by knowing, loving and serving him, by living in a personal community with him and by him. It exists in the world, and yet has been taken out of the world. The spirit is destined to build up the world as intended by God, but by that very fact to constantly disturb the existing world—and naturally every being capable of rebellion against God—as in its self-sufficient and domineering way it strives to draw the spirit within its sphere.

Here lies the element that particularly runs into danger as soon as we segregate the concept of spirit from the revelation of the Holy Spirit who provides its environment: the ability to comprehend the living God; the ability to be addressed by the personal God and to answer him; the immediacy with God, so that the spirit cannot be absorbed by the world; finally, upright striving in the world, as a real being sent into the reality of the world.

If the fact of revelation is lost sight of, the spirit is rationalized, naturalized, functionalized and degraded in other ways or, on the contrary, it is defied and exaggerated.

Once this point has been assured, however, then all the other aspects with which the philosophy of spirit concerns itself attain their significance. Above all, that the spirit is immaterial, that it is simple and immortal; then, that it has a relation to idea and value; that it can manifest itself in activity and order; that it can understand objective activity and objective order, read their meaning, take them over and continue them in a responsible manner—these and all the remaining determinations are true and correct, but only if spirit is rightly understood. Failing that, the spirit deteriorates into the abstraction of Idealism or becomes the counterplayer of blood and soil, as viewed by Nietzsche, or in some other way suffers in its essential destiny.

VII

It is this spirit that sustains human freedom as well as the unchangeable element in man.

This is the spirit which has an immediate relationship to God and is subject to God's call, whose very existence should be an answer to that call. This is the spirit which is not of this world, but is called to perform its duty in the world—a world threatened by the spirit, and yet awaiting it and incomplete until it does its service to the world—not as an autonomous demiurge, but in obedience to God. This spirit sustains freedom. Indeed, freedom is nothing else than the manner in which the spirit acts. Its manner of action is determined by the fact that it does not belong to the world, that it does not have its ontological basis in the world, that it is "higher" than the world, above it, or "lower" than the world, within it, depending on the direction of the interior act by which this fact is experienced: that every spirit has been named, for it was created in a naming act of God. By reason of all this, it possesses a vantage point from which it can decide and choose in a sovereign manner. Thence comes the possibility for the final product of the act of freedom: "I will because I will."

The spirit is a named being; it is *this* spirit. It is not simply one of a genus, but unique. The divine creative act by which spirit came into being was an act of naming. God gave it being as a unique entity. Hence the phrase, "I cannot do otherwise," by which it expresses itself, differs diametrically from the compulsion which makes a member of a genus what it is. The latter is pervading necessity, since the case is determined by universal law. The former, on the contrary, is the expression of a single eventuality in which the unique being becomes one with itself.

And only because it is spirit can it realize the immutable, the factual as well as the necessary, in a manner that characterizes human existence in contrast to the mineral and the plant and the animal.

The natural being simply suffers necessity. The immu-

table takes effect on it, permeates it. Man, too, with part of
his mode of existence is a natural being. To put it more precisely, he, too, exists in nature and has nature in himself.
But with the deepest elements of his being he is not
"nature." Thus he must make a decision. He can permit
natural immutability to affect him—which is then a purely
natural happening, something dead, something bound, lacking even the univocal and self-evident character, the "purity"
of the simple natural process. In that event there is degrada-
tion, an overcoming of the higher by the lower. Or, on the
contrary, man can assume nature to himself from the
vantage point of the spirit. Then he affirms it as the
environment of his being; as a living part of his existence;
as an obligation; as the sustaining basis and the stuff of his
activity; as the mélange of sure instincts and laws. At the
same time, he regards nature for what it is: danger, destruction, violence; something demoniac opposed to the spirit and
to its destiny. Thus he attains the power to assume a
genuinely human position with regard to nature: simultaneously to utter his "yes" and "no" to it; to consider it as
a prerequisite and as an obligation, as a sustaining basis and
as a danger. Hence comes the power to obey it and to
conquer it, to relinquish it, to disengage himself from it,
and again to enter into it and to fashion it.

Here resides the genuine realism of relationship to the
world, equally removed from capitulation to nature and
from an idealistic or dualistic separation from the world—
not in the form of a synthesis or a *via media,* but as the
proper, primary, vital, truly concrete attitude, of which those
others are mere splinters.